Mishaps and Misadventures
When Getaways Go Awry

COMPILED AND EDITED BY
SUSAN CHEEVES KING

Broken Arrow, OK

Scripture references marked CEB are taken from the *Common English Bible*. Copyright © 2001 by Common English Bible, Nashville, TN 37228-1306. All rights reserved. Used by permission.

Scripture references marked ESV are take from *The Holy Bible, English Standard Version*. ESV® Text Edition: 2016. Copyright © 2001 by Crossway Bibles, a publishing ministry of Good News Publishers. All rights reserved. Used by permission.

Scripture references marked NAS and NASB are taken from the *New American Standard Bible*, 1995 Copyright © 1960, 1962, 1963, 1968, 1971, 1972, 1973, 1975, 1977, 1995 by The Lockman Foundation, La Habra, CA. All rights reserved. Used by permission.

Scripture references marked NIV are taken from *The Holy Bible, New International Version*®, NIV® Copyright ©1973, 1978, 1984, 2011 by Biblica, Inc.® Used by permission. All rights reserved worldwide.

Scripture references marked NKJV taken from the New King James Version®. Copyright © 1982 by Thomas Nelson. Used by permission. All rights reserved.

Scripture references marked NLT are taken from *Holy Bible, New Living Translation*, copyright © 1996, 2004, 2015 by Tyndale House Foundation. Used by permission of Tyndale House Publishers, Inc., Carol Stream, Illinois 60188. All rights reserved. Used by permission.

Royalties for this book are donated to World Christian Broadcasting.

MISHAPS AND MISADVENTURES
WHEN GETAWAYS GO AWRY

ISBN-13: 978-1-60495-095-3

Copyright © 2024 by Grace Publishing House. Published in the U.S.A. by Grace Publishing House. All rights reserved. No part of this book may be reproduced in any form or by any electronic or mechanical means, including information storage and retrieval systems, without permission in writing, except as provided by U.S.A. Copyright law.

Table of Contents

Introduction 5
1. *Timeout in Tennessee* ~ Glenda Ferguson 9
2. *Sea, Sand, and Second Chances* ~ Penny L. Hunt 12
3. *From a Flop to a Hit* ~ Liz Kimmel 16
4. *The Cab Ride* ~ Sue Rice 19
5. *Life Without the Tails* ~ Bob LaForge 21
6. *Value in Detours* ~ Pam Groves 22
7. *This Little Light of Mine* ~ Debra Kornfield 25
8. *We'll Laugh About This One Day* ~ Alice H. Murray 27
9. *The Trip Back Home* ~ Patricia Huey 30
10. *God Loves the Lonely* ~ Sandra Johnson 34
11. *A 12 Year-Old Girl at the Beach* ~ Carol Baird 38
12. *Death Valley "Disaster"* ~ Dan Lewis 40
13. *Is Somebody There?* ~ Karen Allen 44
14. *Directive on a Dry Cleaner Tag* ~ Maureen Miller 47
15. *The Creek Don't Rise* ~ Shelli Virtue 50
16. *More than Words* ~ Barbara Farland 52
17. *Bike Ride Thrill* ~ Kim Robinson 56
18. *Rough Rider and the Humvees* ~ Leah Hinton 58
19. *A Three-Week Tour?* ~ MaryAlice Calva 61
20. *Where Are You Going?* ~ Suzanne Dodge Nichols 64
21. *Mission Impossible?* ~ Mary Alice Archer 67
22. *A Lesson in Trust* ~ Judith Vander Wege 70
23. *Tide Pools of Laughter and Loss* ~ Lisa Cole 73
24. *Monkey Jungle* ~ Theresa Parker Pierce 76
25. *Stranded in Tuscany* ~ Jack Stanley 78
26. *Our First Clue* ~ Heather Roberts 80
27. *My True Tent Tale* ~ Kimberly Long 82
28. *A Reluctant Star for a Moment* ~ Lin Daniels 84
29. *Transformation Vacation* ~ Sue Engebrecht 86
30. *Psalm 55:22 Days* ~ Judson I. Stone 89

31. *Better in the Rearview Mirror* ~ Martha Rogers	92
32. *Invisible Baseball* ~ Jill Maisch	94
33. *A Long-Ago Summer* ~ Allyson West Lewis	96
34. *What's My Dowry?* ~ John Leatherman	98
35. *Little Miss Know-It-All* ~ Desiree St. Clair Spears	102
36. *Zing! Pow! Oh No. Not Now!* ~ Debbie Jansen	104
37. *No Rooms In the Inn* ~ Terry Magness	107
38. *Over Before It Began* ~ Beverly Robertson	110
39. *Time Away from War* ~ Cristina Moore	112
40. *Zest for the Fest* ~ Debra Johnston	114
41. *Fried Raw by a Mother's Love* ~ Kenneth Avon White	116
About the Author	120

Introduction

Considering the time and energy we spend on earning the right to go on vacation — extra work to get ahead on all our projects and then planning and packing for the trip — we might wonder if it's all worth it. And even after the vacation begins, we can encounter all sorts of unexpected events. Hopefully these are in the category of "someday we'll laugh about this." Our book is full of such mishaps.

The family I grew up in loved road trips. Some might say that the vacations we took started out as mishaps — or at least with the potential for them. My father, a night owl, did some of his best driving after dark and also didn't like to plan ahead. So, it was no surprise that often we would be pulling into motels with no vacancies and then having to drive on down the road to the next town. By that time, it was usually well after midnight; but even when we finally found a vacancy, my dad would insist on seeing the room before agreeing to stay there.

He was also frugal so on the first of our two five-week-long summer road trips, he arranged to take advantage of a company we'd used before which saves the cost of depreciation because you drive someone else's car.* On this trip, we picked up the car near our home in Southern California and then proceeded to drive it over five days to Washington D.C. After we had toured our nation's capitol for a few days, Dad went to the local company, seeking a car to New York City. When none was available, he shifted to Plan B, which was to rent a car for the trip.

When we were finished touring NYC, our plan was to try again for a transfer car. At that point, if none was available, we would rent a car to Detroit and from there pick up either an ambulance or a hearse (being transferred to a car dealership in the Los Angeles area). One guess what we three kids were rooting for: Plan C, with its amazing potential for extra fun. Alas, it wasn't to be.

Like the others before it, Book XII in the *Short and Sweet* series is based on an idea *The Upper Room* editor Mary Lou Redding caught from a professor at Fort Wayne University. Further inspired by Joseph A. Ecclesine's "Big Words Are for the Birds" (starting on the next page), she started assigning an exercise in classes she taught at various writers' conferences all over the country. It's an assignment I have continued to give writers at conferences for over two decades when I teach them about learning to write with excellent style: Write about something close to your heart using words of only one syllable.

I allow the writers seven exceptions to the one-syllable-word-only requirement. If you see a polysyllabic word in any of these stories, it is because that word fits into one of those exceptions.

If you're a writer — or aspire to be — and the challenge of writing in words of (mostly) one syllable intrigues you, why not give it a try? Contact me at shortandsweettoo@gmail.com to obtain the upcoming theme and deadline.

You could be seeing your own work featured in the next book in the *Short and Sweet* series.

Susan Cheeves King

---

*Designed to transport cars owned by families moving to a new home but not able to drive all their vehicles there, the auto-transfer company pays for any repairs needed along the way and in some cases even pays for the gas. An extra bonus for us was that all the cars had air-conditioning (something our family cars didn't have).

Big Words Are for the Birds

Joseph A. Ecclesine

When you come right down to it, there is no law that says you have to use big words in ads.

There are lots of small words, and good ones, that can be made to say all the things you want to say — quite as well as the big ones.

It may take more time to find the small words — but it can be well worth it. For most small words are quick to grasp. And best of all, most of us know what they mean.

Some small words — a lot of them, in fact — can say a thing just the way it should be said. They can be crisp, brief, to the point. Or they can be soft, round, smooth — rich with just the right feel, the right taste.

Use them with care and what you say can be slow or fast to read — as you wish.

Small words have a charm all their own — the charm of the quick, the lean, the lithe, the light on their toes. They dance, twist, turn, sing — light the way for the eyes of those who read, like sparks in the night — and stay on to sing some more.

Small words are clean, the grace notes of prose. There is an air to them that leaves you with the keen sense that they could not be more clear.

You know what they say the way you know a day is bright and fair — at first sight. And you find as you read that you like the way they say it.

Small words are sweet — to the ear, the tongue, and the mind.

Small words are gay — and lure you to their song as the flame lures the moth (which is not a bad thing for an ad to do).

Small words have a world of their own — a big world in which all of us live most of the time (which makes it a good place for ads, too).

And small words can catch big thoughts and hold them up for all who read to see — like bright stones in rings of gold.

With a good stock of small words, and the will to use them, you can write ads that will do all you want your ads to do — and more, much more.

In fact, if you play your cards right, you can write ads the way they all say ads should be done: in words like these (all the way down to the last one, that, is) of just one syllable.

About Joseph A. Ecclesine

Joseph A. Ecclesine was a Madison Avenue copywriter in the *Mad Men* era. He originally wrote this piece in the 1960s for other copywriters.

A shorter version titled "Words of One Syllable," ran in *Reader's Digest*.

These two versions have also appeared in various other publications while being used as inspirational models for college writing courses around the country.

Ecclesine graduated from Fordham University in 1929, months before the stock market crash that triggered the Great Depression. He was fortunate to find work at the *Bronx Home News* during that period. He later worked in the press department of NBC in Manhattan

While living in New York, he worked at several major ad agencies and became promotion director of *Look Magazine*. His catchy headlines and prose could be found in the campaigns of numerous companies, including IBM, National Geographic, Revlon and American Airlines.

He also wrote fiction and essays. A piece in *Esquire* magazine was followed by work in *The New Yorker, Newsweek* and *Short Story International*. He had an innate curiosity about everything, which translated into an extreme zest for life.

During his retirement in San Diego he taught courses in memoir writing for senior citizens in a continuing education program at UCSD (University of California at San Diego).

~ 1 ~

Timeout in Tennessee

Glenda Ferguson

It was time to leave the Tennessee cabin in the quiet woods. For the past two days while my husband, Tim, played golf, I had been able to relax and find the calm I would need before my busy job as a teacher was to begin the next week.

Tim was in the car ready for the five-hour drive back home to Indiana. This may have been the end of the summer but it was not the end of the heat. He had the A/C on full blast even though it was still early in the day.

"I'll drive until we get to Kentucky. Then you can take over," he said.

Fine by me. After the tasty eggs and toast I had at the lodge, I would be ready for a nap when we got on the road.

While I slept, Tim sped our small car up one Tennessee hill and down the other. But it turned out that our old car wasn't up to the task. I woke up when I felt the car jerk.

"The gauge says HOT. I'm taking this exit now," Tim said. He had a tight grip on the wheel as the car made it off the road. With one last gasp, the car quit.

I didn't want to think the worst, but my fears could get the best of me. Tim knew just how to calm me down. He said, "It could have been worse. We could have been in the middle of nowhere."

I said a quick plea to God for some kind of help.

Very close by were two stores. One had gas pumps. That meant we might find a tow truck. Tim and I were not the type to open the hood and know what to look for or what to do. The other store was a fudge shop. That I knew about — not how to mix up a batch, but how to eat it.

We went to the gas pumps first and told our plight to the guy at the front.

Right then, a man cut in. "We saw your car off the exit," he said. "We noticed your license plate was from Indiana. My wife and I are on the way back." He told us that we might just need a jump. Tim knew that wasn't the case with our car. But he would give it a try. A while later he came back with no luck. They went on their way to Indiana.

Tim asked the guy at the gas pumps, "Do you know of a tow truck we might call?"

He gave us a phone book. This was a time when cell phones were rare, but I had one. Tim did a quick flip through the pages and found two places. I chose one.

"Wait," Tim said, "Let's try Mark back home first. He might know who to call or what to do."

Mark and his staff had been friends with us, and our cars, for years. Any glitch or dent or flat? We knew where to go, and they knew what to do.

I caught Mark at his shop. "It really sounds like your engine is blown," he said, "If you can hang out there for the next several hours, I can come get you when I close up."

What a kind act!

We bought a cold soda and took a trek over to the fudge shop. The sweet smells met us at the door. In glass cases were so many kinds — dark, milk, white, maple, with nuts or nut free. All to salve my sweet tooth.

A woman at the candy case let us taste many types. I bought some of the best ones.

She said, "I saw you from the window when your car broke down. Do you have someone helping you?"

We let her know that our friend from Indiana would be there in seven hours.

Her name was Mary and she said, "You are welcome to stay in here where it's cool. You don't want to be waiting out there in the heat." Mary brought out two chairs from the back. We got to know her and her life in Tennessee.

Every so often, Tim and I would take a walk, but then bolt back to our cool spot at the fudge shop. Mary kept the shop open late that night just for us.

At 8 o'clock, Mark and a friend from his shop made it to Tennessee. "We'll just pull your car onto the flatbed and be ready to head back," Mark said. They took a quick break and got a tank of gas for the truck, which we paid for.

As we got into the back seat, Mary gave us one last gift for the trip home — a huge box of fudge to share with Mark and his friend.

We think of the visit in Tennessee many times — the cabin in the woods, the golf, and the food. But we think about our trip back home even more. That is when God gave us more time in Tennessee. At a sweet spot, we found new friends. As far as our old friends, they went the extra mile to make sure we were safe.

The author and her husband.

~ 2 ~

Sea, Sand, and Second Chances

Penny L. Hunt

CRASH! The end of my granddaughter's long pink pool float sent the wreath on our beach home flying. Shells and sand dollars broke on the porch, and Millie began to cry.

"I'm sorry," she wailed. "I'm so sorry,"

"It's okay," cooed her mother, Laurie. "It was an accident."

Millie's autism made it hard for Laurie to soothe her. "Don't worry. I can fix it." She rubbed Millie's back and pointed to the beach. "Let's go find some new shells to put on it."

"I'll come too, Millie," I said. I'm good at finding shells and know where to find the best ones." I laid the wreath on a table and swept the ruins into a bin.

The tide was coming in as we began our search. Sand dollars and pink shells would soon be hard to find. We picked up the pace, beat the sea, and in no time had all we needed.

"I'll take these home with me while you and Millie go for a swim. I'm going for a bike ride."

Laurie and Millie walked to the end of the beach, where they spotted a pelican standing breast-high in the water and a group of boys throwing rocks at it.

"Hey!" Laurie yelled. "Stop that! Can't you see the pelican is hurt? Leave it alone."

"We're just trying to make it fly away."

"Well, that's not how to do it, and I'll bet you boys know

better." They threw a few more rocks, laughed, and then left.

From an early age, Millie had a rare way with animals. Cats no one could pet would sit in her lap and purr. Llamas at the zoo would shun others with food to be near Millie and touch her hands. And there was Queenie, a Carolina Dingo that didn't come near anyone, but would lie on the grass next to Millie and let her put an arm over her back.

When Laurie told Millie she had a special gift called "animal magnetism," Millie laughed and said, "I have an animal magnet." It's been called her "animal magnet "ever since, and it was working again that day.

Laurie watched in awe as the pelican left the water, walked onto the beach, and sat beside Millie.

One of the pelican's eyes was not closing, and one of its wings hung loose. A crowd began to form around Millie and the pelican.

"What is it?" someone asked. "A seagull?"

"No," Laurie said, taking charge. "It's a pelican. It's hurt and we're trying to help it."

A woman tried to pat the top of the bird's head. It snapped and caught her hand in its beak.

She pulled her hand away and yelled. "It bit me! It bit me!"

"Pelicans don't have teeth," Laurie said.

"Well, it bit me, I tell you. See." She held out her hand with a small scratch on top.

"You must have hit the hook at the tip of its beak," I told her. " You'll be fine."

"That thing's vicious," she said and kicked sand at the pelican.

"Leave him alone," Millie cried as the pelican walked back into the water and out of reach.

"Someone needs to get rid of that thing," said the sand kicker, rubbing her hand.

Someone needs to get rid of you, Laurie thought.

"Millie, we need a towel to help the pelican. Can you hurry back to the house with me to get one?"

"Yes," Millie said. "We'll hurry to help Snappy."

"So, it's Snappy," Laurie said with a laugh, holding Millie's hand as they ran to the house.

When they came back, Snappy was standing in the water. Laurie held the towel high and moved to him. Once again, the bird left the water and sat on the beach next to Millie.

In one swift move, Laurie threw the towel over the pelican and picked it up. It was bigger and lighter than she thought it would be. It snapped at her until she held its beak closed and put part of the towel over its head.

The beach house seemed miles away as she and Millie left with the pelican tucked inside the towel.

Help came when Millie's dad, Jim, saw them.

"Hey, what do you two have there?"

"Snappy," Millie said.

"What's a Snappy?"

Laurie filled Jim in, and he said. "Stay here. I'll get the Jeep and come pick you up."

They left Snappy at home in the bathtub and they drove to meet Travis, a park ranger who worked at the Piggly Wiggly store. He would know what to do.

* * *

Alone at the house after my bike ride, I opened the bathroom door — then closed it again.

Really? There's a pelican in the bathroom?

I took another peek. It was still there, right on top of the toilet seat. As I tried to work out how it got there, Laurie, Jim, and Millie burst onto the scene with a huge box.

All I could say was, "There's a pelican in the bathroom."

"We know," Laurie said. We found him at the beach. He's hurt, and we're trying to help him."

"Snappy," added Millie.

"We have to put him in this box and take him to Travis at the ranger station. He has folks from the Wildlife Refuge Park on the way to care for him."

"How are you going to do that?" I asked.

"I know what to do," Laurie said, and in no time at all, used a towel to move the pelican into the box safely.

We said goodbye to Snappy at the ranger station and, with a stop to buy superglue, went home to fix the wreath and make a late lunch.

The next day, Travis came by to say that Snappy was doing well and would soon be able to fly with other pelicans again. The wreath was hung back on the door, and if I say so myself, looked even better than before it fell.

~ 3 ~

From a Flop to a Hit

Liz Kimmel

When our kids were young, we spent every summer at a camp northwest of Mille Lacs, a huge lake close to the mid-point of our state of Minnesota. Our church friends joined us (or we joined them), for a long three or four days of rest, fun in the sun, boats, walks, and sadly, bugs.

It was a time we all looked ahead to with a great deal of zeal. When the kids were very small, each family unit stayed in their own cabin. But as they grew older, the kids were eager to branch out on their own and stay apart from their folks. So we set up one cabin for the boys and one for the girls. Of course, the door was kept locked at all times to make sure that no one came in who wasn't legit (meaning no boy could cruise into the girls' space and vice versa). This meant that many times a day some not-so-lucky loner would get to crawl through one of the screens to open the locked door so he or she could change clothes, take a nap, or just get out of the sun for a while. If you walked past at just the right time, you'd see two dirty feet slip over the sill and melt into the cabin with only a slight thump as they hit the floor. This was less funny to some than to others.

Every year, this time at camp was filled with joy for all of us, each in our own way. Some loved to slip down the huge slide into the water. Some donned their life vests and swam out to the deep parts of the lake to float in peace.

One year we bought a large blow-up raft shaped like a giraffe. It would hold one big kid or two small ones. It didn't come with the means to steer it, so Dad carved a set of oars out of cedar that were just right for the job. All the kids loved to float about in the raft (all, that is, but one tiny two-year-old who was scared to death of it).

Some liked to fish. Some used the boats to tour the fringe of the camp's Lake Placid (not the one in New York, but the one in Minnesota). Some walked the roads with heads down and searched for rocks. (Lots of agate and quartz would be hauled home after camp was over.) And some of us just liked to sit in the sun and read a good book. Puzzles were a given. Most years we got two or three of them done, many of them being of the one-thousand-piece count. We played board games and ate lots of yummy food. The fire pit was great fun at night, even though the heat and flames didn't keep the horse flies from being pesky.

So many good things to hark back to! But there was that one year when I forgot to pack just about every major thing we would need. Some years the trip was made in June, when there was a good chance that the temps would be warm. But that year we went in May. Back then the cabins had no main heat or air, so you had to add or take away a layer in order to be comfy. Guess who failed to bring any quilts?

Dad and the kids liked to fish, even if all they caught was a baby sunny. Most got tossed back into the lake. Guess who left the lures and hooks in St. Paul? To be fair, I wasn't the only one charged with the task to pack our gear. But I chose to place all of the blame on me.

I brought the Aim, but each tooth brush was back home snug in its place above the sink.

I did bring sun screen — but not bug spray.

We had the cribbage board — but not the deck of cards.

I think the kids packed their own bags, but we parents ended up in the same clothes every day.

I packed the food but missed at least one item from most of the main meals. How did that come to be? What was going through my mind as I prepped for this trip? I should have packed for three meals a day times at least three days. But where was the milk? Why was there no meat for our tacos? Did a food fairy steal all the fruit? How about the corn-on-the-cob? Where were all the snacks? What in the world *did* I pack? I was at a total loss as to what to feed my crew.

I wanted to find a deep hole and sink into it as far as I could sink. I didn't want to face my family and admit to the mess I had made and the wreck I had turned that trip into. I felt alone and was filled with shame.

And then . . . favor came my way. My spouse and kids did not hold me to blame. And my church friends all pitched in to cover the gaps — a quilt or two here, some extra-strength Off! there. And best of all was the open offer from all of them for us to join their tables for our meals. The grace that poured out of them and into us filled my bruised heart and turned a flop into a hit. All four of us found rest in the arms of our dear friends. They did not judge, but looked with mercy on this mom who thought she should just give up and go home. This mom is so glad she didn't.

~ 4 ~
The Cab Ride

Sue Rice

This was our last long trip with our grown kids — a cruise to Barbados, Curacao, Granada, and St. Lucia with a last stop in Caraccas, Venezuela.

In Caraccas, we were warned not to go into town since there had been a coup. But we felt we could not have come so far and not see the city. So, the four of us hopped in a cab and rode into town. I sat in the back of the cab with our twenty-one-year-old son. When I heard a strange sound, I scanned the cab only to see on the roof of the cab a spider the size of my hand.

At once, I was on edge since I knew my son who hates spiders might freak out and scare the cab driver. So I hoped to warn him. When I tapped him and looked up, our son yelled over and over, "Stop the car!" This spooked the cab driver who pulled over and did stop the car. We all jumped out. To our dismay, the cab driver took off his cap and hit the spider, which then ran down the back seat of the car and out of sight.

Our son would not get back into the cab. When asked how he would get back to the ship, which was now ten miles away, he said he would run

back. We asked him to think about the men with guns who lined the streets near the port. In the end, we all chose to put our trust in the Lord and got back in the car. At our trip's end, we thanked God we did not have to deal with the spider ever again.

~ 5 ~
Life Without the Tails

Bob LaForge

I am from New Jersey, but I went to school at Kansas State University. On a trip back home I brought my friend, who had never been out of Kansas, with me. I took him to the shore since he had never seen the ocean. We would walk on the beach and duck sea gulls as they buzzed our heads and stole some of our fries. We got wet sand in our socks.

Then at night, I took him to a fish place where he ate shrimp for the first time. After he had eaten a few shrimp, I asked him what he thought. He said that the shrimp were tasty but they have a bit of a crunch. "Crunch?" I asked sort of at a loss. When I thought to watch him eat his next shrimp, I saw him pick it up by the tail and then throw the whole thing into his mouth. "You know," I told him, "pulling off the tail shell before you put the shrimp into your mouth really improves your eating experience."

All too often we keep at least one or two things in our lives that we should get rid of. For Solomon it was his need for wives. David had his lust. Peter felt that he had to deny Jesus to save his life from harm. And in our own lives, we often have at least one sin that we hang on to even though these sins keep us from fully being able to enjoy the great grace that God has given us. All through our time on earth, God has laid before us a feast of love, grace, mercy, and so much more; but we choke it down with guilt, doubt, and greed. Jeremiah 15:19 tells us to extract the precious from the worthless (NAS). Once we get rid of the hard shell of sin, we can sense the true joy of God's grace.

~ 6 ~

Value in Detours

Pam Groves

My sister, Tracey, and I are now the only two left who took part in our 1964 family road trip to Yellowstone National Park. And I am the only one left who can tell the full tale of the trip. The first feat of the trip was Dad loading our station wagon with camping gear. The second was my brother Scot (age ten), Tracey (age seven) and I (age fourteen) being able to squeeze into the seats filled with sleeping bags. Mom, all smiles, gave us a send-off from the front porch as she waved bye.

As Dad merged onto the nearby freeway, a sound shocked us. "Stop!" yelled Tracey. "Take me home. Take me home now. Mom needs me!" I knew that what Mom needed was a week of quiet mornings on the patio with her coffee and then noon time lying in the sun on her extra-large beach towel. When I told Tracey that Mom had things to get done at home, she burst into angry tears and amped up her scream to be taken home. When Dad didn't get off at the next exit, she yelled, "Take me home now, or Mom will divorce you!" We were shocked that this seven-year-old even knew about divorce and stunned at our usually mild Tracey's yelling to beat the band. I didn't know if I should laugh or cry.

Dad took the next exit off the freeway. No one said a word on the short ride home. When I walked Tracey into the house, I saw a stunned look on Mom's face that quickly turned into a warm smile. Mom's eyes told me, "It's okay" as she hugged Tracey and asked her, "Do you want to stay home with me instead of going camping?" In the warmth of Mom's arms, she softly bobbed her head, "Yes."

Years later when Tracey was a mom herself she said, "I know how disappointed Mom must have been to not have a week to herself, but she never let a bit of that show. The two of us did fun activities together that we usually didn't have time for. It's still a special memory for me."

Scot, Dad, and I made our share of long-term memories that we've talked about many times through the years. A vivid one was from our first night deep in the forest of trees at Yellowstone. It began with swift rain. We were used to heavy rain in Oregon. But this was not an Oregon rain. This pounding rain roared as it fell in sheets. Soon the rain was joined by fierce lightning, as it sought trees to strike.

We sat in the tent and stared at each other. On Dad's face I saw for the first and only time in my life that he did not know what to do. The look quickly left when he firmly said, "Get in the car." By the time Scot and I had our seatbelts on, Dad had the key in the ignition. As we drove away from the huge trees, Dad said in a loving tone, "I'm glad Tracey missed this storm!"

"She would have screamed for Mom, that's for sure," Scot added.

But Tracey might have smiled at our chance event the next day. We were heading to see Old Faithful when we got stuck in a traffic jam on a dirt road. Scot was the first to see the two bear cubs. They rolled down a slope and landed next to our car. They stretched their paws up to the car window. Just as their faces peeked in at us, the line of cars moved and the cubs rushed back up the hill. We were in awe. Did we just see that? Yep. We had proof to show Mom and Tracey: baby-bear paw prints on the car window.

Over the next few days we scoped out buffalo herds, mud pots, waterfalls, canyons, and other signs of nature all around us.

As we headed home, we carried within us all the sights, sounds, and fun.

Over the years when the Yellowstone trip comes up in one of our chats, the three main topics are Tracey standing her ground about going back home to Mom, the lightning storm, and the bear cubs. The fourth topic was our shock when the helpful gas station worker washed the show-and-tell bear paw prints off the window before we could yell for him to stop.

Now when the trip comes to my mind, my first thoughts are of the special gift of sharing time with Dad and Scot as well as Tracey's time with Mom. I have no photos, no souvenirs — nothing that can be held in my hands. And the bear prints may have been washed away, but the time shared became a part of who I am and I think the same for Scot and Dad. It stays with me wherever I go.

~ 7 ~

This Little Light of Mine

Debra Kornfield

I woke up at 4:00 A.M. to the rhythms of Dave's snores beside me and my son's snores in the next tent over. My heart filled with thanks for these two men, for who they are, for the beauty and depth of what each of them gives to those who know them.

On that Saturday morn at Raccoon Creek State Park, the day before our 46th anniversary, my mind reviewed God's great love for us. But for Dave's grit and God's grace, our union would have failed. Our life had been off-the-charts tough for so long — years — that I came close to a break down, long before my PTSD after Karis's death. As for Dave, he had years of depression — the kind where I might open the door to his room and find him on the floor in the dark staring at nothing.

But God . . .

Friday our family had sat around the camp's fire singing fun songs, telling tales, even "Jabberwocky." With our daughter Rachel we sang "This Little Light of Mine," which she had taught her three-year-old Liliana to sing when she felt fear in the dark. Valerie sang the Portuguese, too: "Minha pequena luz, eu vou deixar brilhar . . ." — so right, for when Val was in high school in Brazil, her friends called her "Pequeno raio de luz," which means "small ray of light."

Here's the thing: I could have spoiled this rare camp time. It would not have been due to the hobo meals I had made with the "help" of Caleb and Talita for the ten of us — burnt to a crisp in the coals of Rachel's fire — but from my reaction to this wreck.

They had all taken it in stride and just ate more watermelon and s'mores made with Brian's huge marshmallows. Caleb, Talita, and Liliana laughed as Uncle Dan chased them by our tents. Wee Juliana blessed us with her smile and her joy in both grass and dirt.

But I was so low. Many of my buttons had been pushed — the perfectionist button, the "how-could-you?" button, the "You-are-such-a" button, and even the "Could-this-be-a-sign-of-Alzheimer's?" button.

The author with grandchildren Caleb and Talita.

Oh, I could have made my camp-food farce all about me and in turn stress out the whole group.

But God let me see the family laugh, talk, share what we did have to eat, with a bite or two from the burnt meal. The light of their smiles, each one of them, shone into the dark of my heart and chased the gloom away.

This little light of mine . . . Minha pequena luz . . . like a wall on all sides of my heart as Rachel and Valerie sang in the glow of the camp's fire Friday night. I felt it *still* as I eased through the door of our tent into the dew-grass at the first light of the sky the next day. *Still* — as we hiked through the green woods and the kids swam in the lake. *Still* — as we broke down our camp and said our byes. *Still* — as Dave said "Happy anniversary" to me the next day.

Lord, you give us peace; all we have is from you. My heart wants to praise your name.

~ 8 ~
We'll Laugh About This One Day

Alice H. Murray

My husband and I and our four kids piled into the car to drive to Daytona Beach for a vacation. My mind was on long walks on the beach and being able to read books and take naps. But the harsh truth was I had to ride with crazy folks to get there.

Stuck in a car for hours along a dull stretch of road brought out the worst in my family. While in car jail, all the kids could do was bug me. Each said over and over that they had to eat. Some also were in need of a rest stop, but no two ever had to go at the same time. And they got upset if a sibling had — gasp! —dared to *look* at them.

My husband was just as bad. His focus? The noise from the car's roof where our bags were tied down. Every few miles, he'd stop to check on them. When he did, he said words in a low voice and made weird faces.

It was a hot day, and it was "hot" in the car too. Each of us was mad at one, if not all, of those in the car with us. And the trip was going to take more time if we had to stop at every rest stop from home to the beach and also pull over so often to check bags on the car's roof.

At some point, I'd reached my limit. In a very loud voice, I told the kids we'd stop at the next rest stop. Each one was to go even if they didn't think they had to. My husband would check on the bags while we were there. Our next stop would not be until I said so, and I would take over the wheel to make sure we didn't stop.

Hours later we got close to Daytona Beach, which made the kids perk up and not whine. They began to peer out to try to spot the ocean. Whew! The drama would soon end. Or so I was naïve to think.

We were to stay in rooms on Daytona Beach. My husband had spent time there as a boy, and he'd told me all about this great spot. Yes, the place was right on the beach, but I had to bite my tongue when we drove up to an old house. *This is where we'll spend the next week?* I thought. *I drove hours with crazy folks to come here?* The look on my face led my husband to say how nice it would be once I got past the front door.

All were eager to get out of the car. The kids and I took a walk to check the place out while my husband went to get the key to our rooms. The kids, glad to be out of car jail, ran after lizards in the yard. *Let's just hope the lizards are only out of doors at this place!*

My husband came back key in hand, but he didn't look happy. He said we wouldn't be able to get into our rooms until the next day. Huh? We'd made plans for this date with the owner and paid her before we came. There was a snag, but we could use some other rooms in the house. We would spend the night there and move to the other rooms, the ones we'd paid for, the next day. *Yes, that's how I want to spend my time at the beach — to have to move from place A to place B when I could be in the water, on the sand, or in a chair with a book.*

We took our bags to our rooms for that night. The place was small for six of us. To cheer me up, my husband said we could go out for a quick meal. The kids would stay in the rooms while his teen daughter kept an eye on her siblings. I made a dash to the same car I'd been in all day. But now it was great with no kids to whine or moan.

We took our time with our meal, but at last we had to go back. When we came in, the kids were quiet. Uh, oh. What was up? Turns out a game of hide and seek had led to a lamp being hit to the floor where it broke. We hadn't even been there two hours, and a lamp was toast.

As we swept up the lamp mess, my husband and I sensed how warm the rooms were. Oh, yeah. My husband hadn't told me that the owner said the A/C unit had an issue.

As the night wore on, we felt even more heat. The two older kids left to sleep in our car with the windows down. All I could do was toss and turn. Then, rapid, loud bangs rang out in our rooms. I was in fear that a gun had been fired. My husband found the cause of the noise. He'd put cans of soda in the ice box to cool and hadn't taken them out. They froze and then burst.

To make things worse, my husband found a second source for the extra heat. My young son had found it fun to play with the oven dials. The oven was on, and set to high. Hubby put the dial to off, but it took hours for the rooms to cool.

The next day we moved into the rooms we'd paid for. Our huge window had a great beach view. And it felt cool! While our trip had begun as a bad dream, it ended up a dream vacation.

It wasn't funny then, but what took place on that trip has given us much-loved tales which we've laughed about ever since.

The beach as the author imagined it.

~ 9 ~

The Trip Back Home

Patricia Huey

After thirty-three years in Washington State, my husband and I felt the need to move back to Alabama. We'd soon leave on a road trip across the U.S. to search for a house there.

"I have an idea," I told my husband, Steve. "Let's turn our road trip across the U.S. into a vacation."

"I've always wanted to see Mount Rushmore," Justin, our son, added. He'd planned to move with us.

Steve shrugged. "It might take the full two months to find a house. It's hard to find one in Alabama."

I laughed. "Not many would move to Alabama, would they?"

"You two jot down a list of sites. We'll plan to see at least one or two." Steve paused mid-thought and looked at our six-month-old lab. "I hope we can make it work with Liberty along!"

Just before we left for our trip, we drew straws to see who would sit in the back with the dog. I lost.

Liberty was thrilled to go, but after a few miles, she got bored. I pulled out a toy. Then a bone. Then a snack. Then water. Wiped the drool off my shirt and jeans. I wondered how far away Mount Rushmore was. I checked Maps. Only eighteen hours to go . . .

Steve and Justin were having a grand time up front as they talked about all they'd do in Alabama.

I stroked Liberty. She would do best with a mate. But with the move, there was no way we could take that on just yet.

I spied a sign for a rest stop with a dog park.

Steve took the exit. Thrilled, Liberty dragged me to the park, where dogs of all sizes played.

Too soon, it was time to load up. We'd driven a mile or so when Justin said, "What's that smell?"

"Whew, that's bad!" Steve said.

I looked down. On the floor was a dark mass of fur with rice on it. The rice seemed to move.

"Oh, no!" I screamed.

"What's wrong?" Steve shook his head.

"Maggots!"

Justin looked around. "Yup. They're all over that dead rat. I guess Liberty hauled it in. Better pull over, Dad. Mom, swat them off your jeans."

My jeans? The vile things were on me! I screamed again, then jerked off my jeans, pulled my legs under me, and glared at the dog as she sniffed at the rat.

"There's no place to pull off, Hon! You'll have to deal with it until the next exit."

Stunned, I flailed away at the nasty grubs.

At last, Steve was able to pull over, and Justin purged the Burb of the nasty things.

Wary, I put my jeans back on. "Hey," I said to Justin, "let's toss a coin to see who rides up front!"

"Naw, I'm good."

"Oh, come on. Be a sport, Justin."

"Okay, fine. Heads."

I flipped the coin. Tails.

I lost again.

Back on the road, I checked Maps. Only fourteen hours to Mount Rushmore.

Days later, we pulled up to the Alabama Air B&B, our home for the next few weeks. Right away, we made a plan to find a house.

The next day, we dropped Liberty off at Doggy Come Play, then met with our realtor to begin the search for our dream home. As we looked at homes, though, we saw that every For-Sale sign also screamed Sold.

If we found a house soon, we could enjoy a few sites on our drive back to Washington. We still had to load and move our things back there, but first we had to have a house. We prayed that things would work out, but homes proved to be scarce.

A friend called. "Want to take a break from the house search and go to my craft group? Anna King will be there. She used to go to your old church."

"I'd love to!"

At the craft group; Anna and I, along with others, caught up on our lives.

"How's the house hunt?" Anna asked.

"Not good, and we must head back to Washington soon."

"I have a realtor friend who'll find you a house. I'll text her."

Within an hour, my phone rang. It was Diane, the realtor.

"I have two homes. One is on a busy road, so I doubt you'll want it. The other is small, with fresh paint. Has a nice yard."

"Steve and I drove to look at the house. It looked great with fruit and nut trees. But this area was one of the oldest in Alabama.

Just then, a brown flash streaked past us. "Whose dog?" I asked the realtor.

She stalled. "I was about to tell you, uh, that's the dog that goes with the house."

"What? The dog goes with the house?"

Diane held up a paper. "Says right here, 'No dog, no sale.'"

"Well, I've never heard of that!" I said.

We walked inside the house. Cozy with fresh paint and new floors. A porch fan.

"We can make this work," I told Steve.

He wasn't so sure. "Patty, this isn't what we had in mind. It's in the wrong area. The house is tiny! Maybe we should wait." Steve looked worn out, though. I sure was.

"It'll be gone fast once it hits the multi-list!" Diane said.

I looked at Steve. His eyes spoke.

"We'll take them both," I said.

Months later, we sat on our porch in Alabama. Liberty and Tripp, our dog that came with the house, played in the yard. A butterfly lit on an Azalea bloom. The cicadas hummed. We felt at peace.

A verse of Scripture came to mind.

A man's heart plans his way, But the Lord directs his steps. (Proverbs 16:9 NKJV)

We had thought our 2022 trip across the U.S. had gone amiss. But not in the eyes of the One who had paved our way.

~ 10 ~

God Loves the Lonely

Sandra Johnson

"Good news! I just heard on the radio about a cruise to the Bahamas. I've just charged the trip on my credit card. In the day, it's all you can eat. At night, we get to hear songs from praise groups." My eyes met Deborah's frown.

"You plan to take a van to the airport, get on a plane, change planes twice, land in Miami, and take a car to the pier. Just you?"

My friend crossed her arms with a frown stuck on her face.

For my part, I placed my hands on my hips. "Yes, Jesus and me," I said.

"Yeah, but what if you get lost, lose your bags, and get sick?" she said, with care in her eyes.

"It'll be fine. I have the funds and the time. God is on my side. Be glad for me."

It was 4 A.M. on the day to leave. The sun was not up yet when the van got there. I sang a tune in my head as I climbed in with a pack on my back, and a purse. I tied a scarf to my case so I could find it with ease in the claim area. I slid over on the hard seats and turned to look at my new friends who mouthed "hi." Soon small talk began. One lady with long hair said she planned to visit her kids.

A man with dark shades tried to sleep. As for me, I was wide eyed. I couldn't sleep as in awe I thought of how great that day was going to be, the day I asked God to go with me with the thought, *He will never leave me nor forsake me.** The cruise ship came into view. I moved to the edge of my seat, set to spring out of the car when it stopped.

As I leapt out onto the pier, the prayers began again. *God, help me meet a friend. Amen.*

A man who worked on the ship threw my bag in with the other bags. I heard folks in K-LOVE t-shirts, screech as they hailed old friends. *I'm on the right pier.* The crowd surged into a loud room built to hold large groups of people.

Each group of chairs held a flag with a color. Each mate got a colored band for their wrist. Then the staff told us to wait for a color to be called. Those with that color were to take the ramp up to the ship's deck. I took a deep breath and walked into the room to snag a seat. I told my brain to calm down. When I scanned the first row of chairs in my Blue Zone, I saw three ladies, crammed close, who laughed and hugged as they talked. All three had glasses. All three had short gray hair. All three had a streak of purple on their hair and wore the same t-shirts. My gaze was glued to their t-shirts: God made us sisters, but Prozac made us friends.

A warm surge of peace welled up in me. *Are these the friends God plans for me to meet? I see an empty chair next to them.* "May I sit here? Love your t-shirts." With a huge grin, they said yes and began to nod toward the chair next to them. I couldn't help but

35

laugh. "I'm Christine. I'm from Wisconsin."

"I'm Leila, I'm from Michigan."

"I'm Kathy, I'm from Texas."

"I'm Sandy, I'm from Arizona. "

"What brings you three to this cruise?"

"Each year we drive here and meet on the ship, where you can eat all day and praise all night," Kathy said in a Texan twang.

"How long have you done this?"

"So far, three years," Kathy stated, and stuck out her chest with pride. While we waited for our color to be called, I learned that Kathy was a stay-at-home mom, Christine a nurse, and Leila a preacher's wife. My heart flip-flopped as I heard each sister's truth. I shared about my nurse career and the loss of my twin. I leaned over and spoke in a soft voice. "Girls, I came here with just me. May I join you for mealtimes and the shows?"

"Of course!" Kathy said. The other sisters bobbed their heads.

"I'm so thrilled," I said. "I asked God to help me find friends to be with, and I'm pleased how fast God hears my prayers." Tears welled up. Close to me, the preacher's wife reached out and rubbed my back. She saw the tears.

"I was speaking to the class on my second-to-last day as a nurse professor," I began, "and one student dared me to splash purple on my gray hair for the last day of class. I know God has brought me to you. I see purple in your hair. God is good." I tasted the salt of my tears. Kathy jumped up to give me a hug. I held on tight.

"Blue Zone, please board at this time through the door marked 'Gangway!' " At the same time we heard the ship horn blast. In mid hug, we cringed, and nerves made us shake, as we grabbed our gear and climbed the ramp. In line for food, Christine pulled a spray can out of her purse and began to spray my hair purple. Folks near us gasped, moved three steps away, and began to point.

But all I could think was, *I am their new sister!*

For the rest of the cruise, we were known as The Sisters with Purple Hair.

And I was even more sure that God loves us. He knows what we want before we ask. He feeds the birds, dresses the lilies, and knows the number of hairs on our heads— even if those hairs are purple.

*See Matthew 6:24-32, Luke 12:7

~ 11 ~

A 12-Year-Old Girl at the Beach

Carol Baird

The buzz at home was that we were to make a road trip to a place where we could have a great time of fun in the sun. I thought about how I would laugh and live out my dreams. I'd planned on the drive for my mind to be free and my thoughts to come true. At aged twelve, I thought I knew what life was at its best.

First Mom, Dad, Gram, and Gramps went to load the car full of our goods. After they filled the gas tank, we were good to go. We set out for Ocean City, Maryland. The plan was to meet up with Aunt Lois and Uncle Chuck and their kids. The drive was long, and we were tired. When at last we came to where we would stay for the week, I went off to sleep in a strange bed that would be mine for six days.

The next day, the men got up at 1:00 AM to go out to the bridge to bait traps with small fish. There were no worms, as the bait was for a salt water catch from off the bridge. They drove back to the Villa Nova Cabins to eat a meal of eggs and ham, then drove back to the bridge at 6:00 A.M. to cast their rods and hope for the best catch of the day. Mom and I stayed back to clean up and get set to go off to the shore by noon to swim in the surf and play in the sand.

I was not quite a teen so not quite as vain as a teen girl. Still even girls of my age make plans to show off what they think boys look at in girls. So I just had to show the way I could fill out my swimsuit. A plan formed in my mind that I could not shake. I would stuff my swim top with foam pads.

My tube bobbed on the waves as I lay back and shut my eyes. As I caught a look on a cute boy's face, my heart soared. Just then, a sponge pad popped out of my swim top and began to float by. I could just die. My face turned beet red as shame rose in me, and a tear fell from my eyes. My pride lost, I swam back to the shore on the verge of an all-out cry.

A towel lay wide on the sand near my mom, so I took the chance to lie down to soak up the sun and get a dark tan. My eye caught a gross sight, and my head turned right. What I saw was a girl walk by with a swimsuit top that was like a bra. But the gross view I saw was lumps of fat that burst from the sides and back of her top.

I asked my mom if I had sides and back like her. Mom said, "No!" Mom told me I was young and ate right. I felt shame for her. It was clear to me now. I didn't want to look that way in my swim top. That was not for me. No. No, I did not want to be like her. Why did I think I should?

I had my fill of shame for one day.

Once we were done at the beach, it was time to go back home and cook up the fish catch of the day.

The men came in with their crop of fish. Gram got out the oil to fry them. Dad took out a game board. Rest came for the old folks.

It had been a full day, a good night, and when night came near, our eyes closed, and all said, "Good Night."

The break of dawn brought a new day. The day before, life at the beach gave me a peek at where I went wrong. I had a hope that on this new day I would have a chance to break free for a new dream — one that would not bring shame but joy.

~ 12 ~

Death Valley "Disaster"

Dan Lewis

It began as a dream that became a nightmare which God used to show us his glory!

The idea was sparked when my wife, Michelle, and I were on a date weekend. My mother-in-law had our two boys — then ages six and nine — so we could enjoy some kid-free down time. While we were having a brew at a coffee shop, we saw a big RV pull into the gas station across the street. Thus began a conversation that seemed like a dream: What if we bought an RV, and I took some time off work while we toured America as a family? Michelle was homeschooling the boys so they could take school on the road. And I could save up some time off — as long as I planned ahead.

With that dream in mind, we started to think, plan, and pray. A few years later, in mid-2013, we took the plunge and bought a thirty-one-foot RV (and a Jeep to tow behind it). Even though I did not know how to drive a vehicle that big, I could learn. And we knew we could do a few "test trips" to work out the kinks. Our goal was to hit the road in Spring 2014, which gave us six months to get ready.

In November 2013, our test run took us from our home in San Diego to Death Valley National Park. It seemed like an easy trip — mostly freeway driving and not a lot of twists or turns.

Piece of cake!

Or so I thought . . .

As it turned out, this "piece of cake" trip was a nightmare!

Less than a mile after we left, a car drove by us honking his horn while pointing to the back of the RV. We pulled over on the side of the road to see that our Jeep was being dragged at an angle, the tow bar tweaked and bent.

A few hours after we fixed that, we stopped to get a gas fill up, only to find out that the steering wheel of the Jeep had locked up so that, even though we had fixed the tow bar, the front tires of the Jeep had been locked in straight mode for the whole trip (which meant they dragged around turns and curves) — very bad for the tires.

Add the fact that RVs drive much slower than cars, and the extra time it took at those stops to fix problems, and we were hours later than the time we planned to reach Death Valley. This meant we were going to drive through the middle of nowhere in total dark. And since our trip was at the same time as the New Moon, we had no moon to light our path.

Oh the joy . . .

As we stopped to eat in Baker, I was beat! After a drive of many hours, we still had hours to go before we made it to camp. For a brief time, I thought I would just park the RV in a dirt lot, sleep the night there, and then head home in the morning. This was going to be the end of our grand RV dreams. It was time to give up.

We grabbed some food, talked about our options, and prayed about it. Michelle and the boys wanted to keep going. My nerves were frayed, and I was full of worry about what other blow to our plans loomed on the two-lane road that was the next leg of our trip.

But Michelle had an idea. As a family, we liked to listen to "Adventures in Odyssey." These Bible-based children's dramas were fun and taught some good life truths. What if we played some "Adventures in Odyssey" as we made the last leg of our trip? It could help ease the mood and turn my mind away from all the danger I feared might lie ahead.

We prayed again, smiled at how crazy this day had been, and put in some Odyssey CDs. With that, we went up the dark road toward our final stop.

When we finally made it to our camp site around 10 p.m., it was pitch black. All was quiet.

After a twelve-hour drive fraught with trial after trial, I felt so down that not one thing had gone right. To say I was tired would be an understatement. To say I had lost sight of our RV dream would be the total truth.

But, as I stepped out of the RV, I was met with a grand sight: a sky like no other I had ever seen. Stars filled the night sky. The Milky Way was in full splendor. No mountains or trees blocked the image that flowed on and on into the distance.

I stood in awe as I took in this tour de force of God's glory.

With no moon or city lights, God showed off His vast universe and breathed fresh life into my weary soul.

To this day, that star-filled sky is still burned into my mind as how big and creative God is. Of course, as He tends to do, God taught me a wise truth that night: Though at times the trail can be filled with traps and snares, what God holds in wait on the other side will be great!

As a matter of fact, as I thought more about it, it hit me that God's starry sky had been over me the whole last leg of that trip. I just hadn't seem it since I was busy looking only at my trials.

If I had just looked up, the view of that night sky would have told me that our magnificent God was over us the whole time. (How can I not use a big word for such a big God?)

~13~
Is Somebody There?

Karen Allen

The plan was set for Labor Day weekend. My husband, our two dogs, my sister-in-law Cindy, and her husband Jerry, along with their two dogs, would meet at the log house I found for rent in north Georgia. My friend Kathy, who lived in Georgia, would join us a day later and stay in the extra room.

We all brought lots of food to share. The dogs loved the space both in and out of the house with its room to run, fetch, and play. The house was great. It even smelled great. As soon as I walked in the door, I sensed the odor of pine and cedar in the air. The fire pit was stocked with wood, and the huge grill was ready to use. The L-shaped sofa in the den was plush and soft, and the kitchen was well laid-out. I loved the old metal tub the most. It filled with water from two spouts — cold water on the right and hot on the left. Ah, the joy of a good soak! We each found our niche in the house.

The log house.

As we prepped for the night's meal, all at once the sound from the TV got very loud. We were stunned. It was not just loud; it was very loud. My husband and sister-in-law grabbed at the remote and each tried to turn it down, but it wouldn't work. It took a while to bring it back to a low level. Yet, soon after, the TV did it again. And again! Three times. We didn't know what to think since no one had touched the remote. The TV seemed to have a mind of its own. That was the first strange event.

As the night wore on, we heard two knocks at the front door. My husband went to open the door. No one was there. Weird. We heard it twice more, the next times on the side of the house. Then the knocks moved above our heads. A hard pound came as if a heavy thing had been dropped. This caused my husband to pull down the attic cord and mount the steps to take a peek.

Nada.

Day Three was the light-switch event. It was late at night, after twelve, when the lights went off, then came back on. No one had touched the switch. We didn't even know where it was. In a panic, we tried to find it. At this point, things were quite odd. Too odd for my taste. All these wild things seemed to occur at night. Why was that?

With eyes open wide and nerves on a knife's edge, I went to bed. I'd had a troubling thought come to mind: *Could there be an evil force in this house?* At first I could laugh, but this was now too much. Our fun time away from home with in-laws and my friend was less fun now. My mind went to the verse in Ephesians 6 that tells us our struggle is not against flesh and blood, but against the rulers, against the powers, against the world forces of this darkness, against the spiritual forces of wickedness in the heavenly places. That was it! Dark forces were in our midst, but God was with us, too. I found peace in that thought and was soon able to drift off to sleep.

After a hike the next day, we grilled hot dogs and made a fire in the pit. We fixed a few s'mores as we laughed and talked. I was glad my in-laws had the chance to meet Kathy. She and I had met on a church music trip the prior year.

When it was time to leave, we packed up the food. I saw that some of the bars of chocolate were gone. I asked if one or two had been eaten, but no one would fess up. Even though the second box was open, no extra ones had been eaten. Four bars were gone, and no one knew a thing about them!

After we each packed our cars, we said our 'byes and drove home. When we got home, I got a text from Kathy: "My dogs loved the hot dogs. Thanks."

"What hot dogs?"

"The two you sent home with me," was the reply.

"I didn't send any hot dogs home with you. Maybe Cindy did."

I had to know, so I called Cindy.

"Not me," she said. "Could it have been the ghost?"

~ 14 ~
Directive on a Dry Cleaner Tag

Maureen Miller

At first, all was fine.
We flew from our home in North Carolina to Cancun, Mexico. It was a dream trip with dear friends — a time to soak up sun and catch up on sleep. Though the news had warned of the chance for spring storms, our hearts were filled with hope, so we thought all would be well. The rain and winds would stay far from us.

Once checked in, we and our friends were led to our rooms. Soon clad in swim gear, each of us was eager to sit in the sun — a cold drink in hand — and take in the sights, scents, and sounds of the ocean. The sound of a cello on the air caused us to breathe a sigh of relief.

Our trip had begun.

But in no time, before we could even leave the room, truth knocked on our door in the form of a small, Hispanic woman. In a hushed tone she warned, "All guests must leave at once. They will not tell you this, but 'tis true."

Could it be?

Fear crept in like ants up one's spine. What were we to do? Where would we go? And our friends?

My husband, Bill, stood in a long line of guests to wait to place some phone calls. The grim news had spread, and a strange sense loomed over us.

While Bill worked to get us all out of Mexico, I perched on the bed in our room. All I knew to do was pray. *Dear God, You are Lord of everything — the sun, the stars, and . . .* I felt my voice crack. *And of all storms too. Please, please help us, Father.*

It was a plea. Still, though I was gripped with fear, I knew He was close by. And I knew just where to turn.

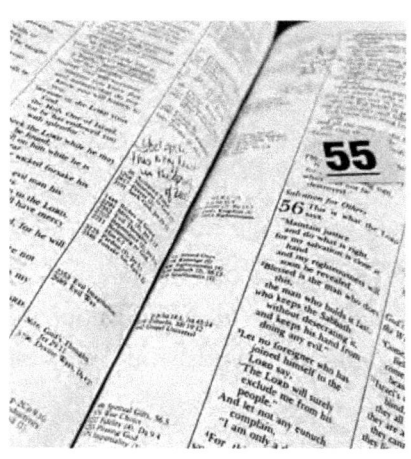

I reached for my Bible, but what should I read? No real plan, I closed my eyes and sort of flipped to a page. There, stuck in the book's crease, was, of all things, an old, gray, dry cleaner tag — with "55" in bold, black print.

I'd turned to Isaiah, so I thumbed through, then stopped at Isaiah 55. Perhaps in that text there'd be a clear word from the Lord, a sign of hope.

I read the chapter aloud, from verse one. When I neared the end, I knew. God would help us flee from the storm.

At some point prior, I'd marked the words, which stood out with red ink. They had brought hope in the past, and they brought hope once more.

"So is my word that goes out from my mouth: it will not return to me empty, but will accomplish what I desire and achieve the purpose for which I sent it. You will go out with joy and be led forth in peace" (Isaiah 55:11-12 NIV).

True to God's Word, and Bill's hard work, we were soon on a plane bound for a new place. Far below, we saw dark clouds which hung like smog over Cancun. Though we prayed for those who'd stayed, some with no way to leave, our hearts soared.

And when we touched down in Nassau, Bahamas, we breathed a sigh, then praised the One who, just as He'd said, helped us go out of Mexico with joy and led us forth to *Sandals Royal Bahamian* . . . in peace.

Amen.

~ 15 ~
The Creek Don't Rise

Shelli Virtue

There's a common phrase used in Kentucky when about to do a thing: "Good Lord willing and the creek don't rise." In other words, you'll do it if not stopped. After being in the state several times over the years, I can fully grasp the need for this phrase.

Our first mishap took place while driving the ups and downs of the hills through that state. We were a young couple at the time with two small kids in tow. Little did we know the police loved to set speed traps at the base of these steep hills to catch cars that picked up speed as they would coast down. So, along with many other naive tourists, we were caught in their trap and had to pay a hefty fine. This was our first bad break in the state of Kentucky.

Our second time through the state, we made sure to be aware of the speed limit and the speed of our RV at all times. We weren't going to get caught by the troopers this time. But again, the creek rose a bit. This time, we had four kids in our care. As we enjoyed the view around us, our RV began making grisly sounds. We limped our way to an auto shop. They had the part to make the repair, but it took about six hours. We couldn't find much in the small town to keep four kids busy for very long. After all, it had never been our plan to spend part of our trip stuck in Kentucky.

From that time on, the family joke was that no future road trip would ever allow for a jaunt through the state of Kentucky.

Alas, our kin did not get the memo. Many years later, a caravan of family members was driving through Kentucky on their way to visit us before moving to a new town. While stopped at a rest area, they called with an update on their ETA.

Our son made a comment that they should get out of the state fast — but not too fast. About a half hour later, we got a call that they had been in a horrid wreck. This time the Kentucky creek had not only risen (figuratively) but it had also spilled over its banks! Their truck and trailer were smashed, so we got on the road to help pick up the pieces and drive them to our home. Our kids were on pins and needles at the thought that we'd have to go to Kentucky to get them. Our rescue mission was a success, but we've never been to that state since then.

I'm sure there are many fine things about Kentucky, but the Good Lord willing, the creek will never rise and float our boat that way again!

~ 16 ~

More than Words

Barbara Farland

"Just one hour to go," I chimed to my car mates as we neared the western edge of South Dakota. "Next stop: the Badlands."

So far, our first road trip as a family was off to a good start. At the wheel was my husband, Terry. Our nine-year-old daughter, Nina, was in the back seat, and I was tasked with maps and plans and all things to get us from here to there. Nine hours on the road can ruin the best of friends, but at this stage in the trip, Terry, Nina, and I were still at peace with each other and thrilled to be on the go. Our plans over the next week would take us to the Badlands, Mount Rushmore, Crazy Horse, Deadwood, and a rodeo — all of the sights and sounds for which the Black Hills of South Dakota are known and praised.

As our car moved west, flat land soon gave way to the roll of hills, then to the Badlands' red, gray, and tan striped spikes and buttes. All looked dry and void of life on this vast stretch of rock, just rock. But, wow, what a sight! What grand proof of a great God who made the world around us! And to think our family would have a chance to look at and live in this scene for a whole two days. It was bound to be a great start to our week of fun and rest.

As we checked into our hotel, a worn sign above the desk caught my eye:

NIGHT SKY PROGRAM

9 P.M., CEDAR PASS AMPHITHEATER

"So what's that about?" I asked with a nod as the man slid our room key to me. He glanced at the sign.

"Oh, it's a must see while you're here. Don't miss it. You'll learn all about how the Badlands were formed, the things that lived here long ago, plus they get out big telescopes to look at the moon and the stars. I think Venus, too."

"And it's just down the road?"

"Yep, not even two miles to the north of us."

I turned to Terry and Nina. "What do you guys think?"

"Sure, I'm game," said Terry.

"Yeah, sounds cool," said Nina.

So it was set. That night we would find a quick bite to eat, take a swim in the pool, then head to the amphitheater when the sky grew dark. It wasn't long before we sat with other Badlands guests from California, Pennsylvania, South Carolina, even Australia. The park ranger used a fob to turn on a projector. A bright scene of fish and sea filled a screen set in the cove of the theater stage.

"So here's how the Badlands looked millions of years ago," said the ranger. "And over the next forty-five minutes, we'll learn about some of the life forms who made their home here at that time."

Click. The next slide showed a mosasaur with a whip of a tail and sharp, deep mouth. The ranger shared fun facts about what it ate, what it chased, and what it feared. The next slide: a nimravid, which looked and lived much like the wild cats of today. The next: some kind of swirled-shell snail. The ranger told grand tales of fight or flight, floods and fires, and the lives lost to the hard tests of time. But as she tried her best to hold the ear and eye of the crowd, more and more people turned their gaze away from the stage and raised their cell phones to snap pic after pic after pic. As time passed, some people even left their seats.

The ranger smiled. "Well, I think I'm done here," she said. "Go ahead. Please take it in."

The rest of us sprang up to join the ranks lined along the far side of the amphitheater. More phones blinked on. The sight of the night sky just couldn't be topped.

Sure, the last rays of the day's sun put on quite a show to our west, but it was the sky to the east that held all of us in awe. Between the tall peaks of the Badlands' spires rose a full moon.

The huge gold orb turned the rest of the sky into rich blues

and slate grays. Thin wisps of cloud sliced through the light. The rock below bore a soft and airy glow.

The hymn "The Love of God" by Frederick Martin Lehman came to mind as I gazed up at that sky — a sky like none I'd seen before and may never see again. The third verse played in my head:

> Could we with ink the ocean fill,
> And were the skies of parchment made;
> Were every stalk on earth a quill,
> And every man a scribe by trade;
> To write the love of God above
> Would drain the ocean dry;
> Nor could the scroll contain the whole,
> Though stretched from sky to sky.

Try as we might, we could never fill the sky with all the love and praise due to our God. But His great love for us was easy to spot in the height and breadth and beauty of a bright moon on the rise that night. Truth be told, God's love is easy to spot every day and even in every small thing if we are open to the gift of it, if we train our eyes and hearts to know it.

I reached for Nina's hand. I leaned into the curve of Terry's arm. Here we were with no words to match the scene. Here we were in the midst of a God whose love note to us stretched above and between us. Our words fail when we try to voice all that God was and is and means to us. In the end, we show our love for Him best when we just stand in awe of Him.

~ 17 ~

Bike Ride Thrill

Kim Robinson

When I was in my early 20s, I pedaled twelve miles to work by bike. I loved to race cars in the dense El Camino Real morning traffic. I had no fear as I cut in and out of lanes and wove onto sidewalks. In fact, any place I could fit, I went.

One day, I thought to take a trip to the beach. That meant I had to cross the California Coastal Range. I wanted to fly down that road. What fun!

I wound up the steep, curved lane, with no thought for the cars by me. The road had no bike path, but I didn't care. I wanted to go over the top and soar down the other side. Once I crossed that peak, I banked the curves with more and more speed, wind pulling tears from my eyes. The thrill made me yell with joy.

All at once, a valley opened before me, and the road hooked a sharp left with its hill. I turned my wheel and leaned into the curve, but a strong wind grabbed me and my bike and lifted us. I didn't turn as the road and hillside veered left. I plunged off the side of the cliff into open space, over a deep valley.

I was flying, all right. Through mid-air!

In shock and fear, I braked, but of course that did not stop me. I didn't dare look below, as I felt myself slowly arc down, gravity doing what it does best.

This was not the thrill ride I had planned.

Then, I was saved.

The mountain came back around the valley and brought the road with it. As the hills cut off the wind, I dropped onto the road and braked to a stop, right when I should have crashed into the hillside. As I stood over my bike, my knees shook while my hands gripped the handlebars. I was in shock.

Just then, a black car full of tourists came by — all talking at the same time and with their cameras aimed at me. I was not pleased; I just wanted them to go away. They drove on. Did they get a shot of my Evil Knievel stunt? I'll never know.

After my bike flight, I was alive by a sheer miracle, a kiss from heaven. It reminded me of Psalm 34:6: *This poor man called, and the* L*ord* *heard him; he saved him out of all his troubles* (niv).

That ride cured my love of speed.

After a quiet outing at the beach, I rode home with more care than I ever had up until then. I bet those who shared the road with me were glad.

~ 18 ~

Rough Rider and the Humvees

Leah Hinton

At one point in my life, I drove an old Ford Expedition we had named Rough Rider after Teddy Roosevelt and his band of brave men, known for their daring during war. I gave it that name in hopes that my children and I would do crazy, great things in it as a family.

It was close to fall in Texas which can be a rare thing as we often shift from July-like heat to cold rain with little to show for the in-between times.

I loaded the SUV with toys, snacks, and CDs so we could sing along on the drive.

We had a place in mind for our quest: Killeen, Texas. My son chose Killeen to see the army base and buy his very own knife from a military store. He was out to spend the birthday money he got a few months prior. My daughter chose every museum between here and there. Other than that, we didn't have a real plan. "Stick with me and I'll show you how it's done." I told them, full of years of trip know-how.

Our only rules for our family fall get away were that we would stay off interstates when able. We would stop to look at all the things any of us wanted to see without pause, and we would visit as many small towns as we could. We also wouldn't eat at any fast food from a chain joint except for the rare dip cone from our road-trip-ice-cream fave, Dairy Queen.

We drove south on Hwy 174 out of Burleson thru Cleburne, Rio Vista, Morgan, and Meridian. Then we took Hwy 6 to Hwy 2602 — Mosheim to Gatesville.

My inner map is pretty good. I can find North in the dark in the middle of a field. But I don't know my way through a small town in Texas without a map. At this time, Mapquest on my Garmin was a new thing. As pilot of this trip, and with no one over the age of eleven to read the map, Mapquest/Garmin was my trusty co-pilot. This dash-mount device was how I would get us from point A to point Z and allow for all the stops in between.

Mapquest led us over back roads out of Gatesville, Texas. By this time, we were not far from Killeen and what was then known as Fort Hood (now Fort Cavazos).

Late in the day, I was sleepy. I had put in hours in the car and hours out of the car to count cows; visit state parks, museums, and town squares; pick up rocks; look for fossils; and walk along late-bloom-thistle-lined train tracks.

Upon leaving Gatesville, things got a bit hazy.

Old Texas roads tend to run together. Barbed wire, Texas sage, dirt road. Rinse. Repeat.

We took Old Strawmill through fields to West Range Road. Passed over Owl Creek, Clabber Creek, Hargrove Creek, Cowhouse Creek.

Who knew Texas had so many creeks?

As I drove down an old two-lane rock road, Mapquest/Garmin said turn right. I did so and drove for a bit more.

After a few miles my son said, "Mom, what does that sign mean? A live — what?"

The sign read DANGER — LIVE ORDINANCE.

Two more signs made it clear we were not where we were supposed to be.

We kept on our path. I had put my trust in Mapquest/Garmin.

And it did its job. It got us to the army base.

Two helicopters flew over and back in broad sweeps above us. It was plain to see we were the focus of their flight.

Trucks sped over the open road and blocked our path.

Army MPs (military police) got out of camo Humvees and ran up on us, guns in hand. (My kids were never scared, so don't fret.)

Here I was, a mom with a car full of kids, out for a quick overnight trip in our old Ford in an area we could not be in.

The MPs asked how I got there in the first place — and I couldn't say. I did no more than what my dash-mount map told me to do. I don't know if we were ever near a range-impact area. I'm sure they would not have told me if we had been. I just don't think danger signs would have been in a safe zone.

Oddly, it seems no one knew that entrance was there. No one knew how Mapquest/Garmin could show a way onto the army base that the army wasn't aware of. The open part in the fence off the rock road was news to all the MPs and the base high-ups too.

After a quick Q&A with high-ranked folks, we were given an escort off the base through the main gate.

By the time we got to the army store, it was closed. I found a motel for the night. The next day, my son bought his knife, and my daughter picked out an army sweater with a patch on the sleeve.

It was a good trip. We did what we set out to do. Even if we had an issue or two with MPs, helicopters, Humvees and high-ups at Ft. Hood, we still got to tick the box for many items on our quest list. My kids thought it was neat.

They still tease me about my sneak attack on a major U.S. Army base.

But you have to keep them on their toes, right?

If you think this is funny, ask me about the time that same old Ford broke down in front of a Federal Reserve Building and the police thought I was there for a heist.

~ 19 ~

A Three-Week Tour?

MaryAlice Calva

My husband, Mike, and I had to fly to Turkey to pick up our new boat. Her first trek was just a short jaunt so that we could check out her sails and rigs and in every other way make sure that she was ready for the sea. Aside from our family of six, we had a crew of one — a Turk who had done some work on her prior to our launch. At the end of the day, we had sailed for hours in the area and were drained. Our hired guy was also tired, and when we asked him to help us moor the boat in the inlet just off the coast near his town, he was also angry. But he helped as fast as he could. Then he took the ship's only skiff and left for town to relax with friends at the local bar. The rest of us took naps.

A short time later, I found water in the salon that I couldn't mop up. As soon as I thought I had it all, more would seep in. When I woke up Mike, his first thought was to ask, "Is it fresh or salt water?" It was salty. That meant there was a hole in the ship, and we had to search it out. We found that the motor was five feet under water. Since there was no way to fix it while we were still at sea, we had to get off the ship. But our Turkish guy had taken the only means to do so. Six of us were still on board, four of them our kids, and we were one-hundred-fifty feet from shore.

We had to do what we could — and that was to bail water. The kids piled up all the pots and pans, and we formed a line from the ankle-deep water in the salon up to the deck. To help us all bail at the same tempo, I sang the first song that came to mind. "Jehovah, Jireh, my Provider. Your grace is sufficient for me, for me, for me." We all sang and bailed, and sang and bailed.

It didn't take too long for folks on shore to catch on to the fact that we might need some help. They saw how low the boat was in the water. They saw the six of us pour pan after pan of water over the rail and back into the sea. Soon the whole bar came out to watch. In no time at all they were in their boats, on their way to save their guests who were in a pinch.

The first man to board our boat was the only man in town who spoke English. He said, "Hello, friend. I know this boat. We'll take good care of you."

A pump was found. The ship was towed to shore. Turns out, the part that our crew had "fixed" had not been fixed right. It now formed a two-inch pipe through which the sea poured in. The next thing was to deal with how wet the whole ship was. It all had to be dried out — floors, walls, sheets, shelves, motor, and more. A friend from the next town over came to help. It took two days to take it all apart, dry it, fix it, and put it back the way it was. The cost: $1,000 in U.S. cash.

The Kara Ada, anchored.

That is not the kind of extra money that we have ever had to draw on, and our Visa cards were safe with friends at our next stop in Italy. But years ago God had known this day would come, and He began to work on a way for us to deal with it. He had told Mike to form a fund, and only God could tell him when to use it. Every so often, when we had an extra buck or two, we would tuck it into this fund. We never took time to count it. A few times over the years we got the go ahead from the Lord to give some of it away.

We had brought it with us on our trip to Turkey.

We held the boat bill in one hand and the God Fund in the other. Then we prayed. God said it was okay to use it at this time. We thanked Him for His plan to save us in our time of need. We looked to Him with trust and knew He would take care of us. We sat on the bed and began to count. There were ones, fives, tens, and twenties. The final tally: $1,000 in U.S. cash, the exact total of our bill. No more. No less. God knew what our need would be, and He made a way. That was the last day the "God Fund" was ever used.

Our plan was to spend what time in Turkey it would take to be sure the ship would make it back home to the States. As it turns out, that time was over a year. What began as a fun family trip of maybe a month turned into a good chunk of our lives. Yet the time did not go to waste. We were changed. We grew. We bonded. We learned. We met new friends. We told many of those new friends about our God. We learned that there is no bind that God can't fix. And so we trust in Him.

~ 20 ~

Where Are You Going?

Suzanne Dodge Nichols

We pulled into the Newport News Campground about 4:00 P.M. on Day Two of a ten-day tour from North Alabama to Kentucky. At this stop, my husband and I were eager to spend the next five days with our son and his family near Newport News, Virginia.

A map from the camp office marked our site. Signs along the leaf-strewn path served as our only guide to Site #16. Sticks and leaves popped and crunched under the tires as we rolled through the woods.

We found Site #16 above a nice view of Lee Hall Reservoir. But, try as we might, we could not make the spot work in a way that felt safe and solid. Sunset would soon be upon us. We made the hard choice to go back to the office and ask for a new site.

As we wound our way out of the woods, the path turned into a paved road along the back of the office.

"I see no place to park this rig," my husband moaned. "I'll have to take us back to the front and park where we checked in."

He kept to the road then made the turn with his sights set on the right-hand lane. Shocked, he saw there was no cross-over to the front of the office.

He was faced with a choice — stay in the right lane to the exit and merge into the 5:00 P.M. highway rush-hour flow, drive until he found a place to turn and start back, or go the wrong way a few yards and make a tight turn to the front of the office.

He chose the short route.

As he took us to this wrong-way roll, a car turned off the highway onto the camp road. In a panic, my husband rushed his plan. He jumped the curb, dug ruts in the grass, and rode up on the sidewalk. The truck's front chrome tapped two trash cans. We stopped with a jolt as the cans spun out of place. By the grace of God, our brand-new camper missed being scraped along a large pine tree.

Shamed and mad, my husband growled, "Well, that was a dumb move!"

He jumped from the truck to look at the mess he'd made. He put the trash cans back into place, and went into the office to admit his deed.

The lady was kind and gave us the go-ahead to set up on any open site not claimed.

In my husband's choice, I could see my own life's paths. I, too, have felt panic in the face of a crisis. I've often tried a shortcut to my goals as it seemed the best way to avoid the heavy, rush-hour flow of worry and self-doubt. I've jumped the curb and dug deep ruts in the ground of dear relationships when I've rushed to judge or speak. At times, my walk of faith has left me shamed and mad at my own dumb moves.

Then I seem to hear God ask, "Where are you going?"

When I admit my wrong, He is kind. In His mercy and grace, He brings me back to the right path — His good path.

The crazy start to our five days at Newport News Campground did not ruin our time in Virginia. We spent each day with our grandchildren and their mom and dad. We toured old sites built long ago, climbed a lighthouse on the coast, and shared a picnic lunch on the beach as we watched a battleship glide into port. Our days were filled with fun, food, and mirth. Every path we chose was good.

But the next time we went to visit our loved ones in Virginia... we stayed in a campground on the other side of town.

~ 21 ~

Mission Impossible?

Mary Alice Archer

As a naïve girl of 18, I was sent on a family mission. The mission, as I chose to accept it, was to go get the family car from northern California and take it back to southern California. My older brother, Mike, had taken it from my parents' home to his new job in Yosemite.

I chose to accept, not knowing what was in store.

It began with a long ride on a Greyhound bus from San Bernardino to a dusty, dingy depot in the dusty, dingy town of Fresno, California. This was where I was to find my brother. I was met by the dad and mom of Mike's friend, John Stark — who also worked at Yosemite. They drove me to their home where I would meet up with John, Mike, and the car. I would drive Mike and John back to Yosemite, visit for a few days, and then drive the car home.

At least, that was the plan.

Hours passed as I sat in the Stark's home to wait for Mike and John. When they didn't come, the parents saw that they were stuck with me for the night and tucked me into their bed couch. At about 1:00 AM, I woke up to my grinning brother and his friend John. Because it was so late, I climbed into the car in my nightgown — since I planned to sleep on the way to the park.

I didn't take note of the chain of beer-can pop tops draped around the rear view of the car.

We drove through Fresno until the guys chose to stop for smokes at a liquor store.

When John and Mike came out, they began to argue, and they kept it up as they got back into the car and began to drive.

All at once, the car braked with a squeal!

As I sat up in the back seat, John and Mike opened their side doors at the same time, shut their side doors at the same time with a loud slam, and took off in opposite ways down the street.

All was quiet as the car slowly kept going until one front wheel rolled up over a curb.

All stayed quiet as I sat in the back of the car. I knew if I just sat in the car for a while, they'd be back. They wouldn't leave me alone in dusty, dingy Fresno at 2:00 AM. They'd be back.

At last, after twenty minutes more, I grasped that maybe they wouldn't be back.

As I climbed into the driver's seat, I saw I was in luck since the keys were still there. The bad luck was that I had no idea where I was, where the guys were, or where the house I had just come from was. Lost, alone in my nightgown, a small sob left my lips as I began to drive around.

Fresno is one of those mixed-up cities with many one-way streets — large, four- and five-lane one-way streets. It seems that it's a local fad to drag race on those streets at 2:00 AM. I found this out after many wrong turns; at each I found five cars coming at me at high speed while honking their horns. I always found a driveway to dodge the drag-racing cars just in the nick of time,.

At last, I spied an open gas station and a kind attendant unlocked the "out-of-order" restroom for me to change out of my nightgown and into some street clothes. He also gave me a tip that, perhaps, I should take down the beer-can pop-top chain and hide the case of beer we found when I opened the trunk to get my clothes.

With more soft sobs, I climbed back into the car — to drive I knew not where — until I saw that the street I was on had become a highway onramp. Just before I reached the highway, I yanked the wheel to turn into a bus-station car lot. I went inside to choke out my tale (okay, this was before Helen Reddy's "I am Woman").

John's parents were not in the phone book, but I thought the street where they lived might be called Grant St.

An attendant looked over a street map with me and showed me where to find Grant St. To my great relief and surprise, I found the street, and while I drove down it, I saw John's parents' house! I knocked hard on the door with my fist, sobbed out my story to the dazed Starks, and fell once again on the bed couch.

At some point later that night, John and Mike ran into each other and said — once again at the same time — "Where's Mary Alice?!" and, "I thought she was with you!" They then got into a fist fight, after which they were arrested by the police and then let go. Mike thumbed a ride to Yosemite to go to work. John thumbed a ride home, where he found me.

Mike was late to work and was fired. John went to work and quit because Mike was fired. (Does that make any sense?)

In the end, we all went home to Rialto, California in the same car, at the same time.

I think my guardian angel was working overtime on that trip.

Mission Improbable? Mr. Phelps, if you only knew.

Mary Alice and Mike in better days.

~ 22 ~

A Lesson in Trust

Judith Vander Wege

Let's all sing Christmas songs," I said, while our family drove to my grandparents' farm in South Dakota. I would be ten years old soon.

"Well, you know I can't sing," mother said with a smile, "but I love to hear you girls sing." My two sisters and I sang lots of songs. My heart warmed to hear our Dad sing with us.

The Christmas songs touched my heart as we sang of Jesus: "Mild he lay his glory by, born that man no more may die, born to raise the sons of earth, born to give them second birth."* I had said "yes" to Christ that fall.

As I looked out at the stars, I saw in my mind's eye the men who heard the news from on high: *"Today in the town of David, a Savior has been born to you; he is Christ the Lord."* (Luke 2:11, NIV)

I see why they were glad, I thought.

As a small child I had lived with Grandpa and Grandma for two years while Dad was in the Navy, so we had formed a deep bond. I loved to go see them and felt thrilled that we lived close and could spend Christmas with them as well.

"Mama, will we be there in time to eat?"

"Yes, they'll have a late meal for us, dear."

On the way, the car stalled. "Whew! Good thing we made it to this gas stand before it quit," said Dad. "Looks like it's the only one not closed."

"What's wrong, Dad?" my sister asked. "Why did the car stop?"

"I don't know," Dad said. He got out and talked to a man who then looked under the hood. Dad got back in the car. "Says he can't fix it," he told Mom. He gave her a bag of nuts he had bought.

Mom and Dad must have felt sad. They'd worked so hard and had just two days off and it wasn't to sit at a gas place. Yet they didn't act mad. They just passed the bag of nuts to us, and we ate together; snug and warm in the car.

That fall, Mom and Dad had learned to trust God. "Think of Romans 8:28," Dad told us now. *"In all things God works for the good of those who love him,* [NIV]. Let's trust him now."

So we sat in trust. To me, this seemed like fun. What would God do? We were safe and loved. We ate nuts and sang more songs. *It will be fine*, I thought. *Grandma and Grandpa will be glad to see us when we get there.*

I was filled with joy to think about Grandpa. I felt he loved me all the time; he was kind to me and made me feel good. His jokes made him fun, but he was wise, too.

Time passed. Then a car pulled up to the gas pump, (which would have been closed if we hadn't been there). The man, a serviceman on leave, made known his joy to find a place to get gas that late at night. He talked with my Dad and said, "Let me take a look, see if I can fix it."

In a short time, he had fixed our car, and both cars were on their way. The man who worked there went home for Christmas, glad he had blessed two families who would have been at a loss if his place had been closed.

As we drove the rest of the way, I thought of the joy of Christmas — that God was born as a child so He could save us. He grew up just like us. As a man, He gave His life to set us free. Then He came back to life! That was the goal of the story of Christmas, for men could be saved only by Christ's death and new life.

What a thrill to see Grandpa and Grandma as they stood at their open front door when we drove up to their house! Their faces beamed with joy. My heart almost burst as they gave us warm hugs.

That year my grandparents gave me my first Bible, the one I used for years. When I read it, I thought about the way God had used that trip to teach our family to trust Him. In that Christmas trip — as in all other things — God had worked for our good.

*from the carol, "Hark the Herald Angels Sing," by Charles Wesley.

~ 23 ~

Tide Pools of Laughter and Loss

Lisa Cole

When I was young, I went to the beach with my best friend, Shelley, and her mom. It was June, 1997. Such a great time for teens! On the drive there, we rocked out to a Spice Girls CD and were set for sand, fun, waves, and sun — "all that and a bag of chips," as we kids used to say.

On our third day, we asked Shelley's mom if we could go to the Boardwalk to play games. And let's be real — meet boys. The sun had set. A sea breeze whipped through the screened door. It stirred our damp suits that were hung out on the rail to dry. "Sure!" she said, as she picked up her beach read from that day and sat down in the Lazy Boy chair.

Now, mind you, back then, I wore thick-lens specs — the kind teen boys did not find cool. "Girl, ditch them. You'll be fine," said Shelley.

I laid my frames on the oak stand by the bed. "Yeah, I'll be fine," I said. The truth was, with them off, my world was a blur. But still, we cleaned up nice, pulled our hair back in clips, slapped on Lip Smackers gloss, and set off down the beach.

The night was crisp. The tide, low. Waves lapped at our toes. It was so dark out by the waves. Young and free, we laughed; our voice notes mixed with the waves' loud song. "Bet you can't beat me to the Boardwalk!" Shelley sang out.

"As if!" I called back.

And so we ran through tide and sand, until our feet met a pool that looked about an inch deep.

My path was not what it had seemed, though. It plunged three feet! Splash! Time froze; my breath caught, and my heart leapt. My shock turned to mirth as Shelley ran back to help me climb out, wet and cold. We laughed so hard while I dried my face. "I guess you weren't fine," she joked, with a glance at my eyes.

The night would still turn out great. Though my face was drenched in sea and salt, we made it to the Boardwalk, ate ice cream, and had so much fun.

A long time has passed since that night. The tide pools of youth were filled with joy, but what of the tide pools of age? Of love? Of loss? As an adult, I now know that deep wells of grief can hide in what looks like tide pools. They, too, look small at first but grow vast as we get near. Then, with no sign to warn us, we may fall in.

It was June '23 when I last fell into a tide pool. I had just read a short text Mom had sent me the week she died. "I'll be fine," I told my spouse, Kevin. Truth was, with both Mom and Dad now gone, my world was a blur. Mom's last words, still so fresh, tripped me as I ran. Splash! And there I fell right into that pool where the past soaks us until we drown in our own tears. This time, it was Kevin who ran to help me climb out. We hugged so hard while I dried my face.

"I guess you're not fine," he said, with a glance at my eyes. Yet the night would still turn out great. Though my face was drenched in grief and tears, we shared a meal, tucked our four kids in bed, and sat side by side to watch a great show.

In June '97, that tide pool's splash taught me to laugh, to stand, and to shake it off. The wet, the shock — it was all part of a young girl's joy. Yet in June '23, I found that same pool, only now it was carved deep by age and filled with tears. This was no race. It was just me and a long fall into a pit of loss. But at least I knew; these pools, these tides, they change us.

Tides of life all come with dips and twists, laughs and tears, leaps and falls. Each plunge, each slip, each rise, each trip shapes who we are. Some say, "Stay clear of tide pools." But I've learned to hold space for them. For in their depths, I find what's true and what's real. That night at the beach is when I first learned to see it. But not with my eyes — with my heart.

Life's tide pools may look small, but they can run deep. Some pools will hold fun and mirth. Some will hold tears and loss. We will fall in. We will get wet. Yet if we don't face them, they lose their power to shape us. If we do, they'll make us strong. Be they good or bad, we can't fear these pools, nor wade too long in them. If we take a fall, we must get back up. We can reach out and grasp the hands of those we love. When our sight is blurred, we can still walk on — with faith and hope.

~ 24 ~

Monkey Jungle

Theresa Parker Pierce

Our family visited the cousins in Miami, Florida many times over the years. On one particular trip, they took us to Monkey Jungle. The zoo featured every kind of monkey available to view. I was twelve — long and lanky but still very child-like. We had stopped by many zoos without incident — until the summer of 1968.

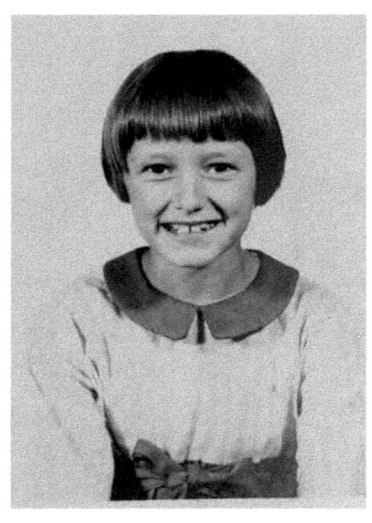

In Monkey Jungle the humans were caged, not the animals. We walked a path through a caged hall to view many types of monkeys in each area. We bought bags of peanuts to feed chimpanzees. I was tall enough to reach up and feed a monkey through the fence holes. They were so adorable. They would reach toward me as far as they could, snag a peanut, and then tear away. It was a great summer adventure.

Then it came about.

After about an hour of feeding many types of small primates, we reached the end of the tunnel cage. Visitors were offered the choice to exit or go on without the cage.

My father and I decided to brave it alone. My father later told me that a sign had warned, "Please hide your peanuts." But I missed seeing it.

Even though things were going great, we were both a bit on edge. Monkeys paid us no mind, but just sat on rocks. It was eerie as they viewed us from afar. Tiny eyes watched us as we moved toward the final exit. One very clever monkey must have spied my little brown bag, twisted tight at the top. He sprang toward me. I lunged toward my father and flung my long arms and legs around his waist. Out of fear, he flinched and flung me off of him. It took place in a flash, a comedy of errors.

I've often thought of that tiny monkey. I am sure he was as scared as we were. After some time we could laugh about it, and now — years later — we still do.

~ 25 ~

Stranded in Tuscany

Jack Stanley

The year was 2010. In honor of our twenty years of being wed, my wife and I went on a trip to Italy where we'd once lived. We met up with a good American friend we'd worked with in Italy and her mother, from Alabama. With them, we had a truly amazing stay in a place we'd grown to love. We spent the week in a villa at the outskirts of Assisi.

On our last day there, a Sunday, we left our friends to set out for the airport. About half the way back to the Rome airport, I stopped to fill up the car with gas so we could return it full. Just after the fill up, as I was paying, I realized what I'd done. I put close to a full tank of diesel in our rental car — one that didn't take that type of fuel! I knew doing this could ruin the engine if I started the car. I went to the small service shop at the Autogrill and asked in my broken Italian if they had a way to take the wrong fuel out of that car, but their mechanics were off, as it was Sunday.

Then I thought about all it meant for that day to be a Sunday. Almost every Sunday in Italy is like Christmas in America. Only a place to buy the basic needs would be open. It's as if every place was Chick-fil-A. I then called the Italian rental company only to find that most of their employees did not work on Sunday . . . anywhere. I was able to get ahold of a tow truck who agreed to take the car to the closest mechanic that had the right tools to take the diesel out of the tank.

We'd left for the airport very early so that on the way we could drop by the hotel where my sister and her fiancé were staying. We'd never been able to meet up with them, but that extra time gave us some breathing space for a visit. At this point, the plans had to change, but we were so glad for the extra time.

The tow truck came, hooked up the car, then headed for a close shop that the rental place had picked. But when we got there, they didn't have a mechanic to work on it because . . . it was Sunday! The rental car place said they couldn't get me a new car but they could come to the mechanics the next day. Now we were down to about two hours before our flight was set to leave.

Since they were in rural Toscana, the car shop also didn't have a rental we could leave at the airport. What were we to do? About this time, a young couple drove up to the shop to see if they could get some help with their nearly brand-new slick Mercedes. They were from Romania, could grasp our English a bit, and also could speak Italian. So I was able to explain our plight so that they could understand. They asked for some time and then walked a bit away to a place where I saw them chat with each other. Then they came back and said in their broken English that they would take us to the airport.

What relief came over us! They helped us put our luggage in their large trunk, kicked in the ten cylinders of that Mercedes, and got us to the airport with enough time to run to our gate (since we didn't have a rental car to return)! Thirteen years later, we are still friends with the only Romanians in the world that we know. Kindness of that type from *anyone* is a clear sign of what is right in the world and that love is the universal language. But kindness on the spur of the moment from total strangers whose language and culture we did not share comes only once in a lifetime.

~ 26 ~

Our First Clue

Heather Roberts

In lieu of Christmas gifts, my family meets each year at a new site in the Midwest. Five families, ten adults and ten kids from age five to eighty-five come together to build memories.

Our first clue that the year's hotel choice might not be up to par was when we were told they did not stock blankets or pillows. My sister had opened her room and found that only one bed had any blanket or pillow. When she went to the front desk to ask, they said they had none. She had to find a maid to scrounge some up.

Our family's room was the only one on the second floor not under construction. Tools screeched all day long. None of those rooms' doors locked at night — the rooms that had doors, that is. Saws, sledgehammers, and other tempting tools for boys to play with were strewn all over the place. Some rooms had gaping holes where windows should have been. I'm happy to say that no one died or got maimed during our stay.

At the pool, while the cousins splashed and played, the adults tried to visit amid the din. Hot beaches and paddle-boat rides filled the days and sunburned, fitful sleep filled our nights. But what stick in our minds the most are the mishaps and near disasters at that hotel.

The last straw came as my sister and I helped my parents pack up and check out from a different hotel, and I got a phone call from my son. "Mom, I don't want to bother you, but is it normal for it to rain in the hotel room? Rain is pouring onto the bed. We packed up everything and put it, by the door. Dad's bringing around the van to load stuff. Don't worry, the girls are safe."

I don't know what I said in reply to my son. But I can call to mind the wave of thanks I felt as a parent that God had kept all the children safe amid so many near disasters. He even held back the indoor rain until the end of our stay.

God is our refuge and strength an ever-present help in trouble. (Psalm 46:1 NIV)

We can see that the Lord comes to our aid after grief and woe. But I think that He also protects us from bad things even before they can occur. I believe He is a God who acts to avert much pain and strife. As a mother of four, I am sure that when I get to heaven, I will learn about all the ways God kept us safe that I never knew about nor prayed for. We serve a great God who stands firm for us, who can't be moved or changed from His path to work for our good.

You can be sure that my husband called the town's fire marshal to report the hotel for all the violations. We did our part to keep the next child who might stay there as safe as we could.

~ 27 ~

My True Tent Tale

Kimberly Long

It was a good plan gone wrong. A girl who loves to camp, I had asked my friend Larry to come along to make me feel safe out in the wilds. I saw him as a help, a guard in the night. So, it was quite a shock when he was the one who turned on me in the wee hours.

I awoke at 12 A.M. on the dot. Of course, it was to go pee. I got up, stepped to the tent door, and bent down to grab the zip. That's when the crazy began.

Larry grabbed my arm and then kicked my gut until I fell to the floor, hard on my rear end. I felt strips of pain start down my arm from the tight grip he had held. I sat there stunned. He had slung his whole self off his mat and lay there still. I called his name. He grunted, then got back on his mat. Shocked, I sat there for a while then lay back down; I dared not try to go pee, no way. As I reeled from the pain in my arm, sleep didn't come for at least an hour later.

You would think that was it, but no. One more time I woke — this time from the sound and the sway of the tent. It was 3 A.M. At first, I couldn't think what this thrash of noise could be but in the light of the moon, I began to see that it was Larry's kicks to the walls of the tent. I called his name and then he quit and was still once more. All I could think was, *What the heck?*

When he awoke the next morn, he didn't know what he'd done or how the tent came to have a hole. And when I told him the hard facts and he saw my black and blue arm, he looked shocked. Then it seemed as if the shock turned to shame. So, we stopped the talk and moved on.

My arm and rear end were both sore and bruised, but more than that my heart was sore for my dear friend who had some deep pains that caused this kind of night agony. He was one of my best friends. I was sure that this man had not even one cruel bone in his body. To all who knew him he was a good guy with a great heart.

I never dreamt it would be my friend to strike in the night since he was the one who had come to guard my life. From then on, I planned to camp alone and just carry a gun — or maybe some bear spray.

If I made it through this crazy night, I thought, *I can handle just about anything that might come my way!*

~ 28 ~

A Reluctant Star for a Moment

Lin Daniels

It was our first ever family vacation to Disney World in Florida. My twin sister, Patty, asked me to join her and the kids (Jen, nine) and (Joe, five). After a three-hour plane ride from Connecticut, we grabbed a taxi and reached our hotel at about 8:30 P.M. I, for one, was ready to sleep! My plan: Go to bed, rise early at dawn, and start out fresh. I had dreams on my mind, and my body said "Amen"!

But Patty had another idea. "The kids won't be able to go to bed. They're too antsy and can't wait to see all that Disney holds."

So off we went to a theme park. Patty, the peppy kids, and the aunt with "zzzzz's" on her mind. The first "ride" we came upon had old TV shows as a focus. As we sat with the crowd to wait for the show to begin, a person who works at Disney began to search for volunteers. Jen and Joe both began to point at me — and kept it up. They began to chant, "Aunt Lin! Aunt Lin! Aunt Lin!"

And that's how I was cast for the role of Lucille Ball in the well-known chocolate-factory clip in "I Love Lucy."

Clad in a white-and-red apron and chef's hat, I was cued each step through the clip. "Take the chocolates fast off the belt!" "Faster, faster!" "Tuck them in your shirt! " "Faster, still!" "Stuff them in your mouth!" And even though a chipmunk might have thought I was a long-lost cousin, I could not keep up with those chocolates!

Even though I did not act well, my bit caused my sister to laugh 'til she cried. With joy in their hearts, the kids had a grin from one side of their faces to the other.

Even thirty-five years later, as we hark back to that night, each one of us smiles.

And to think I was ready to go to bed early and miss the whole thing.

~ 29 ~
Transformation Vacation

Sue Engebrecht

With eyes on the speedometer I wondered, *How could an adult feel so pathetic?* Not only did freeway speeds cause panic waves in me, but every time my husband passed a semi, it took my breath away. Tires spun fear-filled mile after fear-filled mile. This jaunt to meet his cousins in Missouri was about to reveal what a coward the dear man had just wed. Two of his cousins were professors, one a nurse, the fourth a historian . . . and all smarter than this college dropout. Insecurity slid from my gut and kicked neck muscles on its way to pace in my brain. Words from 2 Timothy 1:7 gave me a spark of hope to hold on to: *God has not given us a spirit of fear and timidity but of power, love, and self-discipline* (NLT).

That first night in Missouri, dinner set me at ease. Cousins' stories swung like open doors to welcome me into the family. Mirth knit us together, and love hugged my timid spirit. All was great, until plans to do a cave tour the next day made my childhood fright wail, "You've got to be kidding!" I shushed the fear and prayed for power to make it through the tour.

The three males, all over six feet tall, were not good at dodging stalactites. I took on the role of cave monitor: "Duck. Watch it. Lean right. No, no. Your other right." Turns out the English prof was even more afraid of caves than I. So I held her hand and smiled a lot. Taking care of others left me no time to be afraid.

We were nearly out of the cave. As my attention relaxed, Hubby ran into a stalactite. Head wounds bleed a lot. The nurse in our band took charge.

That night Hubby laid his hurt head on a pillow, hoping for deep rest since he was set to drive us home the next day. Just after 12:00 A.M., I awoke to scuff, hiss, and thump sounds. Like any good wife, I was quick to share the event. My mate was not only slow to wake up, but at first failed to leap into the role of hero. Over and over I urged him to get out of bed and act. At last he rose, trudged to the door, shut it, and said, "There!" He was almost asleep again by the time I said, "There — what? Whatever is out there is still out there." I stared into the dark and prayed for fear to take a hike. Sleep came.

Just after dawn, my hero said he was going down the stairs to make coffee. As for me, I aimed for the shower. About mid wash, a furor arose. Loud voices and sounds like large items being moved urged me to dress in a flash and go down. I found a chest freezer pressed against the bottom step and climbed on top of it. On the other side stood Hubby, holding the back door open. He had a canoe paddle in the other hand. Before I could utter a word, a ball of fur shot into the kitchen, took one look at Hubby, turned toward me, then made a quick right and a dash into the dining room. With a yelp and flutter of the other canoe paddle, the economics prof was close behind. Hubby let go of the door to join the race. By the time I got to the dining room, the wild ones were doing laps around the table. Fur ball peeled off and ran into the bedroom. Two cats on the bed watched as it slid under the bed. Professor shut the door and said, "There!"

I said, "There — what? The animal is under the bed. Your two cats are also locked inside." A plan hatched. Storm windows and chairs became a glass path from the bedroom door to the now-open front door. With a tight grip on his paddle, the professor entered the bedroom. A raccoon shot out and then zip-dashed down the glass path and out the door. I looked out to see the dazed animal in the front yard. I said to him, "The wild paddle men aren't chasing you anymore. You're free little one. Time to go home."

In the house all was calm — for a little while. I saw the face of my dear spouse etched with pain. During the race, he broke his foot. It took some time to sort out a broken foot and the storm windows, chairs, and freezer plus get luggage into the car. At last we were ready to head home.

Hubby looked snug in the back with his bound head on a pillow and his iced foot on the seat. Armed with new skills from the last night's make over, I slid behind the car's wheel ready to hit the freeway and pass a semi or two. Due to God's power and love, and my new-found self-discipline; wild fears no longer chased the new me. A secure woman drove off toward home and left timidity and fear in the Missouri dust.

~ 30 ~

Psalm 55:22 Days

Judson I. Stone

My wife, Jan, and I drove to York, Maine, to see our sons and grandchildren. On a Friday, after ten fun days with them, we set out for the trip back to Florida. Our first stop would be New Brunswick, New Jersey. It turned out to be a Psalm 55:22 day.

The journey south took us through New Hampshire, Massachusetts, and Connecticut. In New York, we turned onto the Saw Mill River Parkway that is just for cars. At this time, the car's battery light came on. I paid no heed to it for a time since the battery was only two weeks old so shouldn't have a glitch. When other dash lights soon came on, Jan checked the car manual. It said to pull out the charge cords to our phones to end a drain on the battery.

I pulled off the Saw Mill Parkway to head for a Honda shop. As we went up a small rise in Chappaqua, the car stalled, but I was able to steer it to the side of the street. It came to a stop in front of the Horace Greely House. I got out of the car and looked under the hood. The battery wires were tight. Jan and I prayed. Psalm 55:22 guided our thoughts and words: *Cast your burden upon the Lord and He will sustain you; He will never allow the righteous to be shaken* (NASB).

I saw a group text from a friend who leads a Men's Powerline prayer group. Here was the chance to make our needs known to the men. I sent the plea and then made a call to AAA to set up a tow to the Honda shop.

Ramon, one of the Powerline men, called from Illinois to pray for us. I shared Psalm 55:22 with him. He prayed while I stood on the sidewalk. I thanked him. Jan and I sent texts to her sisters. Her brother-in-law thought the glitch had to do with the alternator.

I stayed to watch the car while Jan walked to a bagel shop to charge her phone. The staff was very kind to her. My friend Gary, from the Powerline, called from Texas. I shared with him Psalm 55:22 and we prayed. The AAA agent kept in touch with me by phone. I liked her care for us.

The tow truck arrived in less than two hours. The driver let down the truck bed. With us back in the car, he charged the battery. Then he had me drive the car onto the truck bed where we rode on the way to the shop. We saw the road from up high above the road. It felt strange to be guests in our own car as it moved along.

When we arrived at the shop, the truck driver again charged the battery. When the car came on, I backed it down off the truck bed and parked it. With fear, we walked into the auto shop to tell the receptionist that our car alternator had to be checked. My mood soared when I read a sign on her desk: "Jesus is my Rock." She got right on the job.

In the waiting room, I called the hotel and travel agent who made sure that if need be, we could cancel our hotel room with no fees. We were told that the car would need a new alternator and that they could make the switch on the spot while we ate a late Subway lunch and looked at the new Hondas. Car problems can raise doubts about one's car.

I made a new hotel reservation. We hopped back into our fixed car by 6:00 P.M., though we had less weight due to the cash we'd forked over. As we got back on the road. Jan and I thanked God for how our needs were met through the delay and the bill. We praised God for our rainy-day fund.

Our stop in New Brunswick was five hours later than planned, but Jan and I made it into our hotel room by 7:30 P.M. — in time for our reservation.

The next day, on a bright Saturday morning, we met with an Archivist who helped me with my book, *A Modest But Crucial Hero,* about a young missionary — one of my ancestors. A purple orchid was our gift to thank her for her help.

Back on the road, we drove to our next night's stay. Two days later, Jan and I reached home in time to get things in place in case Hurricane Idalia came our way. It did not.

After this car mess, Psalm 55:22 means even more to us. This tale and the power of this Bible verse helped us face the thought of any trip with peace. Our main prayer was for strength and patience, which God gave us at every turn. We feared the worst — missing our Saturday book meeting — but looked to God for the best.

We all have Psalm 55:22 days and can rest in faith that God will "sustain" us so that we will not "be shaken."

~ 31 ~

Better in the Rearview Mirror

Martha Rogers

In February of 1985, not long after we wed, we planned a trip to Korea to see our Navy friends, Rick and Debbie, before my husband, Doug, was separated from the Navy.

As luck would have it, the four of us chose to meet in the Philippines before Doug and I faced the cold in Korea. Being in the military, Doug and I flew "space available" from Los Angeles into Clark Air Force Base. Once on the ground, we took a bus to the Naval base at Subic Bay where we found out our friends' plane had not been able not take off due to icy weather.

We lost the rooms we had booked on Grande Island, and no beds were open on the naval base. In hopes of finding a room elsewhere, we caught a ride back to Clark Air Force Base. But back at Clark, we found out there were no extra rooms for use at all. About the time we began to fear we had to stay in the terminal for the night, an airman found us a room off the base out in the country. The night was pitch black, with no lights along the way.

Our trip to a nearby village was on an open-air cart to who-knows-where. At this point we didn't care. We were so hot and tired, we were happy to just be able to lie down. But we were in shock when we saw our place for the night. The room had a dirt floor with a light bulb that hung from the ceiling. The walls sweat with black mold and the bugs were crawling under us, over us, around us, and on us. The bed was stuffed with hay and chickens ran pell-mell on the other side of the screen door.

Is this for real? we thought. For one thing, we could not drink the water, and a shower was also out of the question. So tired we could not think, we fell onto the bed, which then sank to the ground in the middle, which made us roll on top of each other.

Two hours later, we went back to Clark Air Force Base. Since we couldn't reach our friends, Doug was ready to hop on the next plane to L.A. Finally he was able to talk to Rick. He told us they could meet us at Subic Bay because the weather had cleared.

For the second time, we took the bus to Subic Bay and waited for our friends. When they flew in later that morning, they found that Debbie's luggage hadn't flown with them. It was sent to L.A. so we had to go shop for clothes for her.

Somehow Rick was able to get our rooms on Grande Island back. We stayed two days in a cottage on the beach . . . where Doug got a bad sunburn because I rubbed oil on his back instead of sunscreen.

Rick and Debbie flew home. Manila was the next stop for us, then Baguio up in the mountains where we were pleased to be able to stay in the military recreation center. The nice room and cool air were a glad change.

Later Rick and Debbie flew home. Doug and I took a flight into Kadena Naval Air Station in Japan and then to Korea.

Debbie picked us up at the airport in Korea. Then the real fun of shopping began. Things were so cheap there. We had suits and shirts tailor-made and were even able to buy a queen-size brass bed and rocking chair and ship them to the States. Our shopping trip brought us joy as we bought treasures of every kind. Most of all the four of us enjoyed our time with each other.

We have since shared many more trips with Rick and Debbie. And when we look back at all that went wrong with this one, we just laugh.

~ 32 ~

Invisible Baseball

Jill Maisch

Each summer our family went on a two- or three-week trip so we could camp. My parents, two brothers, and I would pile into our station wagon that was hooked up to our pop-up camper.

Once, while on a long drive through Missouri, we felt a thud and then heard an awful screech. Dad slammed on the brakes and pulled the car to the side of the road, and we all stared in disbelief as a tire from the pop-up rolled on past us.

Dad ran down the road to fetch the tire then steered our car with the maimed pop-up to a gas station close by. As luck would have it, their repair shop was open. We were told it would take at least two hours to fix the dent in the rim and put on a new tire. To help pass the time, my mom thought up a game for us to play. She led us to a grassy area and taught us how to play what she called "invisible baseball."

The rules were the same as the game we all know, but the plays and the calls were all made up. The pitcher would send an imaginary ball through the air and the batter would swing their imaginary bat to hit it. At times, the pitcher called it a strike, but most times the batter would hit the "ball" and run toward "first base." If the hit was a fly ball, the outfielder would hold up their invisible glove, stare at the sky, and lunge to catch it. Most times we agreed with the fielder's call — either an out or a missed catch. Once, when I ran to second base, my older brother ran toward me with the invisible ball, so I slid into the "base." He said I was out, and I said I was safe. We laughed and laughed about being at odds over an invisible play.

At one point, an older couple stopped at the auto shop area to eat their lunch. As they ate, they watched us play. We could tell by the looks on their faces that they were quite at sea as to what to make of it. Once they caught on to what we were doing, though, they laughed and laughed. They even cheered when my younger brother made a make-believe home run. Before they drove off, they rolled up next to us and told us how much fun they had as they watched us play.

My mom's game of Invisible Baseball was a real hit, so to speak, since it made the two hours fly by. When the tire was fixed, we piled back into the car and went on down the road.

Invisible Baseball was a family favorite for years. We played it in many camp areas and in our back yard. At times, others asked to join in. Nothing could be more fun than watching a large group of adults and kids play Invisible Baseball!

Years ago, when our family was stuck in a bog of blah, my mom "made lemonade out of a lemon" with a game that gave us joy for years to come.

~ 33 ~

A Long-Ago Summer

Allyson West Lewis

1996

A summer to look forward to. My sister and I planned it all down to the last item.

Grandmom and Grandad were to drive to Atlanta so we could ride in one car while my sister and her husband drove theirs. We booked a house for a week of bright summer sun. Cousin John, from Virginia, planned to join us.

We were still in the prep stage and at home.

That's when things began to go wrong.

My Ford Bronco got a flat tire. I praised God. "Thank you, Lord, that no harm came to me or my five-year-old son."

My gas stove quit. It turned out to have a slow leak that could have killed us. "Thank you, God, that no one died."

My pet-care girl backed out. As I searched for a new one, I prayed, "Thank you, God, for keeping her safe."

I kept a list of trials before we had even left for that longed-for trip. It came to over fifteen things!

At last, we packed up our two cars and drove nine hours from Atlanta to Cape Hatteras. The house by the sea charmed us all. And it had lots of room.

We loved to watch my son and his two cousins of the same age play all day on the beach. Back at the house, we all bathed the kids and cooked while they played.

Two days had passed when our cousin, John, blew in. Thrilled to have him cook his best shrimp dish, we drove to the store to buy some. John took great pride in his choice of just the right fresh shrimp. But, when all the things were rung up, John turned to me to pay. I smiled and gave the clerk cash as I thought, *Thank you, God, for* all *my blessings.*

Early one day, a man from town came to our front door to tell us Hurricane Bertha churned our way.

We had to leave by noon.

We grabbed the kids and took one last fun drive on the beach in the Bronco. And, of course, we got stuck in the sand! Two young men drove up. I smiled. At last, help had come. They told me I needed to let air out of my tires so I could drive on the sand. Then, off they drove. I looked at my sister and we both cracked up. We did as they said and drove toward the beach house to load up.

We met Cousin John on his way up the drive. He stopped to say "Bye!" and then sped off. We laughed and shrugged. No help from him!

We made our flight from the storm as fun as we could for the kids. While the drive back from Cape Hatteras took a long time, they didn't catch on to the fact that storms like the one coming were not safe. "Thank you, God, for taking care of us."

I had no idea what would come next in *that* span of time . . . or at any time. But what I do know is that till the end of time, I am blessed by God.

Bailey Cheney Birol, Erin Cheney, and Stephen Langford.

~ 34 ~

What's My Dowry?

John Leatherman

My first glimpse of her was at the welcome brunch on Day One of our resort stay in Antigua. With her blond hair in a ponytail and in her green sundress, she looked cute and roughly my age. Thanks to her Club Dream ID tag, I knew her first name was Julie. Learning anything else about her was tough.

"Hi, Julie, I'm John. Where are you from? What do you do there?"

Without lifting her dark brown sunglasses, she replied in a cool, flat tone. "Thank you for asking me what you can read for yourself. The United States. And I work." She turned away, her wide sunhat flapping.

I took the hint. For the rest of my stay, I found others to talk to. I met some nice women — all from Europe. Or New York City (which to me might as well have been another continent). I had fun, but nothing began that would last.

I didn't talk to Julie again until we were at the baggage claim.

Like most of the Americans at the resort, I left Antigua on a Club Dream charter flight to Miami. There, at Terminal E, we would claim our bags, pass through customs, and then go back through TSA for our next flights. With a few other international flights using the same carousel, that first step would take a while. I aimed for a bench to sit on and wait. As it turned out, it was next to Julie.

"I'm sorry, I'll move." I said, as I began to stand up.

"No, no, sit," she said as she touched my arm. "*I'm* sorry. I was cold to you on the first day. You didn't deserve that."

I dropped to the seat as she went on. "It's just, you reminded me of a guy I met on my last Club Dream trip. He was also named John. He came on all sweet and sensitive. But he liked to get drunk, and then he'd turn into a real jerk. I told him to stay away from me, and he . . . didn't take it very well."

"Oh, wow."

"I can tell now you're not like him. I never saw you get drunk."

"I don't get drunk because I never drink." I grinned. "Unless you count Diet Coke."

Julie laughed. "Anyway, I hope I didn't ruin your week."

"No, I found a fun game to play: 'Avoid Julie.' "

She sighed. "I'm sorry."

"Speaking on behalf of all Johns, *I'm* sorry."

"We need to find something else to say to each other." She gave me a silly grin. "Would you ever marry me?"

I winced and then realized she was initiating the drinking game we'd learned at Club Dream. I gave the expected reply, also the name of the game: "What's my dowry?"

"An aging apple. What's *my* dowry?"

"A broken bugle and an aging apple. What's *my* dowry?"

"A crumbly cookie, a broken bugle . . ."

And it goes on like that from A to Z. If you mess up, you take a drink. If someone makes it to Z, everyone takes a drink and the game starts over. It works better with a group. And when you, in fact, have something to drink. So, we decided to just blow in each other's face. And when we found we had travel breath, we switched it to the ears.

We kept the game going even as we fetched our bags from the carousel. We finally had to stop it for customs, but we couldn't stop laughing. The agent processing Julie's passport asked, "Could you please not smile so much? I can't tell if this is you."

Once past customs, we got ready to split up to go to our flights. A steady stream of Club Dream New Yorkers headed for Terminal J, where yet another charter would take them home to LaGuardia.

Gathering my bags, I smiled at Julie. "Have a safe flight back to . . . uh, the United States."

She hugged me. "Yeah. You, too."

My flight would leave from Terminal D. I headed for the tram but stopped a few steps from the curb, sensing something amiss. I had my backpack and rolling tote, but where was my dirty-clothes bag? I'd packed it in a blue duffel for the return flight.

I rushed back to the spot where I should have picked it up, but it was gone.

What should I do now? Does the airport have a lost and found?

I dashed away, tote rattling over tiles behind me. I didn't know where to go until, passing an airport cafe, I noticed a familiar shade of blue.

My duffel lay atop some distinctly feminine-patterned bags — next to Julie, who was sitting at the bar.

I sank onto the luggage stack in relief. "Oh, thank God!"

As if she'd known I would come, Julie set down her glass. "John, are you sure you've never had a drink? If not, maybe you should start."

My breathing slowed as I blushed. "I don't know what I was thinking. Thank you so much for holding on to my bag."

"Oh, you wanted it back? I thought it was my dowry."

"Guess you haven't smelled it yet." I sat next to her. "I thought you'd be gone already. Isn't that LaGuardia flight about to leave?"

"Yes. But *my* flight's not for another two hours. I'm going to Tampa."

"*Tampa?*" I gasped. Not long ago, I couldn't wait to never see her again. Now she'd become sweet, fun, and about two hours south of my home. "I live in Orlando."

"Thank you for telling me what I can read myself." She nodded. "From your luggage tag."

I took great care to craft my next words. "Julie, on the bench, when you asked that marriage question, did you *want* to play a drinking game? Or did you want my honest answer?"

"Let's put it this way . . . ." She fished in her purse for her business card and handed it to me. On it she'd written her email and phone number — along with, "Here's your dowry."

~ 35 ~

Little Miss Know-It-All

Desiree St. Clair Spears

Soon it would be fall, and school would start again. That year I would be in the fifth grade. While I liked school and did well, I wasn't ready to say bye to summer. So far, my family had stayed home the whole time. Mom and Dad were short on cash and couldn't pay for a hotel stay. Then they had an idea. Aunt Rennie and Uncle Bernie lived just a short drive from the ocean. We could visit them and go to the beach. My heart soared!

I loved my aunt and uncle and would be happy to see them. When they had come to our house for Christmas, they had brought me a gift — a notebook. On the front was an image of a girl and at the top a title, "Little Miss Know-It-All." When my mom saw it, she laughed, "That's perfect, because that's who she is!" I was glad they knew I was smart.

When we got to their home, we piled out of the car, and they met us in the yard with a warm hello. While my eyes took in the posy bed in the back yard and the vegetable plot next to it, Uncle Bernie told us how bad the mosquitoes were and urged us to enter the house to avoid them. Yikes! I moved fast!

Aunt Rennie gave a tour of her home and where we would sleep. Uncle Bernie showed us the attic where he fixed clocks. I was in awe. Uncle Bernie was smart.

Aunt Rennie was a good cook. In that first meal she fixed, I tried okra for the first time, fresh grown from her garden. I liked it. She also baked a great cake. She said she used eggs from their guinea fowl in her cake. I learned that I liked guinea fowl eggs, too.

Uncle Bernie liked to tell jokes; Aunt Rennie liked to laugh, and no one had a laugh like hers. Uncle Bernie asked, "What's black and white and red all over?"

"Hmm…" I thought about it. *Maybe a chimney. Bricks are red, mortar is white, and soot is black. That has to be it.* "A chimney?"

"No, a newspaper!"

Then I knew he meant "read" not "red." We laughed, but Aunt Rennie laughed the most. Her laugh made me laugh more.

After our meal, Uncle Bernie got out the paper and gave Mom a part of it so she could work on the crossword. Any time she got stuck on one of the clues, I would butt in, "Let me see if I know it!" I hoped that in time I would get one right.

I bent over the table to look at it, and as I did, I pushed my rear end right through a glass window pane. Shards flew every which way. "Oh, no!" What a mess! I felt so bad. Then it struck me, *Here come the mosquitoes!*

Uncle Bernie moved fast to patch up the hole. Later he would go to the store to get a new pane. As for me, I had pain of my own.

Years later, I still laugh about this event, and when I think about the trip as a whole, I carry a warmth in my heart that will last till my life long.

We did go to the beach and had a good time, but the best parts of our visit were the love I felt and what I learned: Laugh more, and laugh at yourself. Try new things. You'll never know what you like until you try. Learn new things. But keep in mind — you'll never know it all. Do what you can with what you have. Value what you have and fix it when it breaks. Grow things, for home grown is best — most of all, the love of a family. And when pain comes, you'll know who to count on.

~ 36 ~

Zing! Pow! Oh No. Not Now!

Debbie Jansen

I've commanded you to be brave and strong, haven't I?
Don't be alarmed or terrified,
because the Lord your God is with you wherever you go.
Joshua 1:9 CEB

Ron and I shared big grins as we drove down a Tennessee mountain. Our trip plans were hard to work out. They felt like a can of worms. But we were glad to be on our way.

After a night with friends in Georgia, our next stop was Florida. While on a six-lane road with large trucks and cars all going seventy miles an hour, Pow! A tire had blown.

The van shook. I screamed. Ron's knuckles turned white as he tried to hold the van in his lane. Fear gripped us. We were sure we would crash.

"Jesus," I cried out, "help us!"

A space cleared. Ron drove us to the side.

AAA changed out the blown tire for the spare, but the mechanic at the tire shop had bad news. "I'm sorry, Sir. We can't get a new tire for you until tomorrow."

We went back to our friend's house and spent the night. The tire was fixed by 3:00 p.m., and we began the long trip to Florida.

At 9:15 p.m., we were fourteen miles from our family. Once more, we were on a six-lane highway going seventy miles per hour with large trucks and cars. I was in the back of the van when I heard a hiss.

The sound grew loud.

"Ron, what is that?"

First a bump, bump, bump sound; then we began to rock from side to side.

I clutched the seat. "Oh Jesus, help us again."

Zing! Pow!

Oh no! Not now! The breath caught in my throat.

Ron steered the maimed van to the side of the road. In shock, we didn't move.

Not another mishap! Should we have stayed home? Didn't we plan well enough? We had bought new tires for this trip. The first flat had been the mechanic's fault. He hadn't put the tire on right.

Ron looked at the new flat and climbed back into the van. He bowed his head and stared at his hands. "I don't know what we hit, but the tire is sliced. I just don't get it. Why is this trip so hard?"

AAA told Ron they couldn't get to us until morning. We were tired and felt cast off. We didn't want to spend the night on the side of the road. We didn't want to call our eighty-nine-year-old Aunt with more bad news.

I took Ron's hand to pray. "Well, God… here we are once more. We need help. Please help us."

Within a short time, a truck drove up. The logo on the door was *Road Ranger*. The man said hello and went to work.

Then a truck from AAA drove up. "Hi. I saw you on the side of the road and felt you might need help." The two men fixed the tire. They were very kind and gave Ron's soul a lift.

Back on the road we were at a loss for words. We thought about the day and what could have been. When Ron parked in Uncle Lloyd's drive he took my hand. "It's not about what we did or didn't do," he said. I think God wants us to know that we are in His hands no matter what. We must take our eyes off our mess and hone in on God's shield. Worse things *could* have come about, but we are safe. That's His grace and love. We are blessed."

The rest of our trip was the best we've ever had. We had a fun time with our family as we laughed, ate good food, and thanked God for His grace. I'm sure God smiled with us.

~ 37 ~
No Rooms in the Inn

Terry Magness

Some years ago my husband and I left with friends on a trip to fish in upstate Minnesota.

The four of us crammed into our pickup — with boat in tow. We drove for hours from Southwest Missouri with plans to stop for the night in Minneapolis. We arrived only to find that the Minnesota State Fair was in full swing and all rooms were taken. We had no choice but to stay on the road and stop to check at each town along the way.

It grew very late. We were dog-tired and still couldn't find any open rooms. All at once a bright neon sign broke through the darkness — AVAILABLE ROOMS! We were thrilled. At last, a bed! But our joy was short lived. The made-over bar with five motorcycles parked right in front gave us pause. Each of us searched our good sense to ask: *Should we stay here or not?* Our drained frames had the final word. We parked the car and walked in.

Not too bad. At least the lobby was clean. Its center was filled with tables and chairs set for a free pancake breakfast for guests. But as we scanned the area, we saw what were stalls whose thin walls did not go all the way to the ceiling. They lined the front of the place on each side of the door we had just come through. Our faces fell. It was clear, that these were *the rooms*, and there was only *one* left. We were in dire straits.

We peeked in the available "room." It was *very* small. Its two double beds could fit into the space only when placed foot to foot. Aware that we must sleep or would pass out, we chose to *sleep*. Shoes off, we climbed fully dressed into our beds. Sleep came in seconds for all but one who lay wide-eyed through the whole night, as the bright colors of the neon sign flashed in through the window she faced.

We rose early. We tried to hide our brushes and paste as one by one we made our way across the open area, through the tables of guests and locals, to the only bathroom in the whole place. Then, with teeth clean and bright, we sat down to one of the best pancake breakfasts ever. Soon we were on the road.

We made it to our final stop in just a few hours. The next day, after a truly good night's rest, we piled into our pickup-with-boat and drove toward the lake. The wives sat in the back, men in front.

Only a few minutes had passed when I caught glimpse of a sight in the rear-view mirror that took my breath away. With no thought, I grabbed my camera, slid open the back window to the bed of the truck, and begged the driver to stop. Then, I climbed out. My friend trailed after me. The man on a bike whom I'd seen had caught up with our truck. In one hand, he held by the tail a huge turtle the size of his torso. What a sight! I snapped his picture, and then our truck took off, and the man was gone.

We fished the lake, and in a day or two our guys yearned to stream fish. We found a spot that could have been a spread in a magazine — and it was alive with fish. The guys messed with rods and lures while we girls soaked up the quiet beauty. Up ahead, I saw the side view of a man as he stood in the stream. He held an arched rod, and his line danced above the water. Then he turned and I saw him full face. It was the turtle man!

Later, he shared with us that he had been a scientist with the NASA space program. But after a time, he chose to make a bold life change and left the "rat race" and its stress for "the simple life here in Minnesota."

His menu for the week? Turtle soup.

~ 38 ~

Over Before It Began

Beverly Robertson

The waves lapped the shore. Not a cloud in the sky as the Florida sun shone down on the Atlantic Ocean. We basked in the warmth of eighty-two degrees, not like our low of thirty at home at the time. Yet, while the sea breeze blew through our hair in a place where anyone would want to be at such a cold time of the year, my husband and I were on the phone to catch a quick flight back home.

We had left Flint, Michigan with a lot of other folks who sought to flee to a warm place. We had heard of a virus from China, but didn't give it much thought. We were just so glad to board our plane and land in warm Sanford, Florida, and drive to a mobile home park in Vero Beach to spend a week.

We didn't hear any news. Soon I got a call from my daughter in New Jersey. She told us how bad this bug had become. She said we should leave as soon as we could. That night, I heard the President's speech on my cell phone and learned we had to stay in place. This would cost us more than we could pay. We couldn't get stuck there, but had to wait until we could leave.

The Canadians who lived in the park packed up and left. They feared they could not get home.

That night, we went to a great place to eat that had not closed yet. We bought wipes and meds in case we got sick. We headed North to Sanford to catch our flight at dawn. We did not want to miss our chance to get back home.

The next day, McDonalds had closed, and we couldn't find any other place to eat so went straight to Sanford to catch our plane. When we got to our area to board, things were tense. The crowd let out a sigh when our jet pulled up to the gate. We rushed to our seats and wiped them down with Clorox swabs. One man, two seats up on the left, coughed all through the flight. When the plane touched the ground, we got our bags and took a van to the car lot. We climbed into our Eqinox and drove to our small Michigan town. Most of the stores were closed. We scrounged for food in one store with a lot of bare shelves.

Not until we walked through our front door did we feel safe. At no other time did a vacation at home seem so good.

~ 39 ~

Time Away from War

Cristina Moore

This trip was our chance to leave the war for a short time. As troops in a war zone for a year, we were given two weeks on ground — to start as soon as we set down at our end point. Then we would go back to fight in Iraq. My spouse and I had a chance to go to any place we chose. We could go home, but then we would have to say bye to loved ones again. So we chose to go to Australia, a place we had dreamed of going when we were at peace.

But from the start, our trip was fraught with snags. Our flight took us from Iraq to Kuwait to Germany to Dallas and from there to Australia with a stop in Los Angeles. What a trip! Of course more direct flights to Australia could be found, but these were our planned flights. Our flight to Los Angeles was held up so we had to stay the night in Dallas. We had a great hotel with plush robes for us in the rooms. We ate a great meal and saw the night lights of the city. When we made it to Los Angeles, we had to stay one more night. We went to Hollywood and the La Brea tar pits and had a great meal. None of these stops were our end points, so none of these days counted as part of our time off.

We then landed in Australia but with no bags! Since the next day we were to leave on a boat to go dive for a week, the airlines gave us funds to buy new clothes. We shopped and ate and loved our first night in Australia. The next day, as the boat was going out of dock, our bags came with all our stuff. This was day two of our two weeks on ground. We took our dives on the Great Barrier Reef, stayed at Cairns and then saw Uluru. We stayed a night in Adelaide for the best wine and in the end, a last night in Sydney. We flew out of Sydney on day fourteen of our time on ground back to Iraq.

All these snags led to one of the best trips we've ever had. By the end of all our stops, we had spent twenty-four days out of the war zone instead of the seventeen days of most troops. On our dives, we saw sea life that man was never meant to see. It showed us so much of what God made. We saw Uluru and felt one with those who walked this earth before us, those who lived from what our earth alone had to give. We drank wine from grapes that have a mold that grows on them that makes the best wine I ever drank. We saw a green park in Cairns that was the most grand place I had seen.

Full of awe in the midst of all these things, I did not think once about flight delays or lost bags. Not once did I think of war or the heat of the Iraq sun. All these snags led to days not planned, extra stops, and more laughs at all the times we had to say, "You can't' make this stuff up."

God can — and He did. He used the mishaps to give us the best of all times away from war, to show us the vast span of what He had made from land to sea, and to give us twenty-four days of peace and joy!

~ 40 ~

Zest for the Fest

Debra Johnston

We couldn't wait to get to Lake Superior. There'd be a chill in the July air at night. We'd sit around a fire to make s'mores. In the morning, we'd rise from our tent and cook hot cakes near the clear blue waves edged in white.

Close to Rhinelander, Wisconsin all that changed. Our old Suburban chugged and clunked.

My husband, Stan, was stressed. "I think I saw a car repair shop about a mile back. I'm going to see if we can make it there."

Our thirteen-year-old son sat up and then went back to his Game Boy. We had to coast down the highway, well below the speed limit.

Art, the mechanic, found what was wrong and gave us the bad news. "It's your alternator. It will take me a day to get it fixed," he said. "You'll need to stay the night, but you won't find a place for miles. Every room has been booked for months. The Hodag Music Festival is here."

Then he turned and walked back to his shop.

Stranded! So much for a fun trip. In our hot SUV, we had no clue as to what our next move would be. We could have been stuck there for hours or even days.

Art came to where we sat in the shade. "Folks, I called in a favor. A friend of mine owns an RV Park. He said you can camp on his overflow site."

"How will we get there?" I asked.

"Load your stuff in the back of my truck. I'll drive you when I close up. Your Suburban will be good to go by noon tomorrow."

Tent, sleeping bags, cooler, camp stove and tote bags were tossed into the back of his truck.

Art dropped us off at what looked like a ghost camp with its row after row of bare tents and vacant trailers. All the other campers had gone to the Fest for the day. We thanked Art for the ride, grabbed our gear, and then set up our tent.

From the picnic table, we gauged our site. There was not a thing wrong with the RV Park. It just wasn't the Great Lake park we had planned on.

At 6:00 P.M., festival fans flowed back to their tents and trailers. We weren't really alone; we just happened to be the only ones not at the music fest. The camp hummed with joy. One group told us about the Country Music stars they had heard that day. A lady offered to drive us to the fest the next day.

Two campers that stuck out the most were Brad and Greg. In their twenties, they gave us cold drinks. They knew the whole camp, and treated us like friends. Brad and Greg's zest for the music seemed to rub off on us. The night closed out with fireworks.

The Suburban was fixed on Saturday as Art had pledged. We paid Art for his time and thanked him for all his help. Back on the road, we finally made it to Lake Superior where we spent three days of planned peace by the lake.

Twenty years have come and gone. When we've shared tales of our past trips, there's one that we always bring up. It's about our unplanned stop at Rhinelander and the folks who took us into their fold — Art, the skilled mechanic, Brad and Greg, and the fans of the Hodag Music Fest. The best unplanned stop ever. To this day, we still hear Greg's voice, "Brad, bring the beer!"

~ 41 ~

Fried Raw by a Mother's Love

Kenneth Avon White

Some things just aren't meant to be mixed. Think about it. Who on earth would put hot sauce on ice cream? Crazy, right? Or wear plaid pants with a striped shirt? That makes about as much sense as a walk on water with no Jesus there to help! Even worse, and does it really need to be asked, Who on earth would smear baby oil on a fair-skinned child on a hot summer day at a scorched Texas beach? Logic says this mix would be wacky and even a tad cruel. But this bit of beach logic flew right out of the car past our blonde curls blown to bits by winds that raced through Mama's 1963 Corvair. We were bound for Galveston to play in the sun and surf.

Mama's beach party plans, which I'm sure were not meant to turn the party into a pig roast, began back at home as we packed. Did she stow away food and drink first? Uh, that would be a hard "no." Was it a towel for each of us? Can't say that it was. Only one thing made the first cut — the most vital thing of all — Mama's jumbo jug of baby oil. Her view was that the fresh beach air and glow of a new gold hide was a cheap way to set life straight — the reset that we all need from time to time.

At the beach that jumbo jug of baby oil was also the first thing popped out. By birth order we each got doused with the slick gunk — Belinda the elder, then me, then Colleen and on to Doug Jr. — the baby in the house. Once the gob of goo sunk into the depths of our skin, it was at last time for us kids to play. We threw balls of sand at each other until one of us won the fight. Then we took a float on the crest of waves and got swept down the shore like Mama said not to do. We dug deep holes and piled heaps of sand onto each other until body parts were hard to see. When it was time for a break, we ate bread packed with meat and cheese and topped with beach grit that swirled through the air. One hour after we ate, we did it all over again.

Mama felt one hour was the time it took to make sure the belly didn't cramp up while in the water and cause us to drown. When I think back, I guess her worry had good cause. At the age of three, Colleen jumped head first, buck naked into a pool with no means to help her float. Mama flew down the stairs that led to our unit and dove right in — clothes and all.

No, the water didn't kill Colleen, but I could swear Mama could have. As for Colleen, she just laughed and laughed and laughed. But Mama spewed words I would not come to know as "cuss words" for years to come. (If the truth were known, words like these got me popped in the mouth—"in love"—from time to time as I tried to stoke my lingo with new curio verbs and nouns.) I have to admit it; we kids thought that the time Colleen got dunked was kind of funny. As Mama came up out of the pool, she looked like an old worn string mop left out in the rain. After that time, the one-hour rule was put in place lest we cramp up and get washed out to sea.

Just as the sun set, the four of us mutts crawled back into our toxic Corvair wedged side to side. I say *toxic* since this was the same model car Chevrolet put out where carbon monoxide fumes were known to flow back up into the cabin. This left the chance that we'd show up half dead when we got where we were going. We were stuffed in so tight that each of us could feel the body heat of the other. This led to a push here and there to gain more room and that would then turn into a gloves-off fight. With her left hand on the wheel Mama reached back and began to swat each of us with her right.

We screamed in pain.

Mama looked back and her eyes bulged as round as a moon pie. Then she began to whoop and howl. My mind has to grasp at the thought of the exact thing that came out of her mouth but it went along the lines of "You runts are red as beets!" When we hit back as we tried to push away her slaps, she screamed too. Her skin was burnt to a crisp, just like ours! That baby oil might as well have been the fuel and the sun's rays the match that lit our skin on fire!

As a single mom, my mama came up with some novel ideas in her time to get us through. So, I'd like to think our rush to the Piggly Wiggly frozen food aisle was out of love and not a bid to dodge a charge of child abuse. We bent over the cool open vats and stretched out our arms in front of us as if at the altar of frozen corn dogs and pizza gods. This gave our faces and pits of our arms a blast of cool artic air. When the stares began to pile up and it was clear to the Piggly Wiggly boss that we were not there to shop, Mama, in the comic style of a fiery school truant cop, yanked us from the store.

Once home, Mama caked our skin — one by one — with the snake oil she called Calamine. No patch on our body was left bare. She spread that pink goo so thick that our skin turned five times more pink than a Barbie doll's world. The pain did begin to ease, but the tight fit of our clothes made things worst. So, Mama came up with her next novel idea. We cleared every bed sheet shelf in the house and wore sheets as clothes! For an entire week, we had our very own non-stop toga party!

Sure, I can make fun of all this now, but there is a moral to this story: Some things just don't mix — such as kids, summer sun, and a fresh coat of baby oil. To think else is a sure way to get a mother's gifts from God fried *raw* and break a few *laws* along the way!

Back: Ken and Belinda
Front: Colleen and Doug

About the Authors

Karen Allen (p. 44) has a passion for music and ministry. Retired from cancer research, Karen fills her time with writing, caring for her mother, travel, dog walks, club meetings, and missions. She serves as the organist for her church at Meadow Brook Baptist in Birmingham, Alabama, where she and her husband of 41 years, George Parker (Parky), attend.

A breast-cancer diagnosis inspired her to write *Confronting Cancer with Faith* (confrontingcancerwithfaith.com), a Bible study that has brought encouragement, comfort, and hope worldwide. Karen has also published numerous articles, short stories, and devotionals. Her newly released devotional book *Outta My Mind, Into His Heart* provides a unique approach to the mental-health community. Connect with her through her Ewe R Blessed Ministries website and subscribe to her blog at ewerblessed.com.

Mary Alice Archer (p. 21) has worked in education for over 40 years. For the last 26 years she has taught middle schoolers math, English, history, French, art, drama, and science. Now she is tutoring Chinese students online.

She has a B.S. in Exceptional Education from the University of Central Florida. She has written and illustrated two award-winning children's books: *If a Cat,* and *The Christma Cat,* and has published in *Clubhouse Jr.*, and in four previous books of the *Short and Sweet* series.

A Southern California girl for the first 40 years of her life, she then moved to Central Florida. She and John have three children, six grandchildren, two Havanese dogs, a Bourke's parakeet, and a Hermann's tortoise named Melville, of course.

Carol Baird's (p. 38) stories and poems are inspired by her memories and her relationship with Jesus Christ. Her work, including a poem in *Cool-inary Moments* in the *Divine Moments* series, has been published in several anthologies, and as an online devotion in Christian Devotions.us.

She is a member and past treasurer of the Volusia County, Florida, chapter of Word Weavers. Carol writes rhymed poetry, devotionals, and Bible studies and hosted a two-year poetry church group titled Poetry with a Purpose.

Carol is a wife of 63 years, mother, grandmother, and great grandmother. In 1998, she retired from the Corporate World. Card crafting is her hobby. In past years she has taught study groups and workshops, spoken at Women's Ministry, taken part in a lay evangelism program, and worked on a Co-Labor Core during a Billy Graham Crusade.

MaryAlice Calva (p. 61) was raised in rural Minnesota. She married her childhood sweetheart and together they have four children. Some of her life roles include nanny, teacher, pastor, missionary, and CFO.

Having resided in Turkey, Italy, Mexico, and the U.S., she's lived in houses, apartments, an RV (with her four children) and a sailboat (with her children and some of their children). This has led to some grand adventures. She enjoys telling stories and has started writing about some of her experiences so that the fun can be passed on.

MaryAlice is currently active in her church's women's ministry and co-leads a writers' group. She has written curriculum for children's church and Minnesota history, and is working on content for her website, EveryDayPearls.com. Her contribution to this book was co-authored with her close friend Liz Kimmel.

With a pen in one hand and a heart filled with passion, **Lisa Cole** (p. 73) is known for her commentary on the human experience. Her three published books, numerous magazine contributions, and three-year run as owner of an indie publishing house speak to her dedication to the craft.

But it's her role as executive director of Turning Pages SC that defines her. She's not just a writer; she's also an educator, community lover, and advocate for literacy in her home state of South Carolina. Her creative writing, inspired by relationships and the nuances of everyday family life, touches the soul — reflecting an understanding of life's twists and turns with an old-school charm.

Lin Daniels (p. 84) retired seven years ago, after 39 years of teaching physical education, mostly at the elementary school level. Since then, she has enjoyed writing, preaching on occasion, and working with the youth group at church.

An avid golfer, Lin and her twin sister play several days a week. They especially delight in playing as partners and dress almost identically except for one small item (maybe a different-colored hat). After all, their opponents need to be able to tell them apart as they "zig and zag" a bit as teammates. Recently, Lin has found a passion for pickle ball as well.

Lin gives thanks to God for the depths of His love as well as all the surprises He has graciously bestowed on her.

Susan Engebrecht (p 86) writes for magazines and a number of anthologies — including *Chicken Soup for the Soul* — and also writes newspaper columns and devotionals. She's won a number of writing and Toastmaster speaking awards. Susan co-directed and taught at a Christian writers conference in Green Lake and continues at other speaking engagements.

Wisconsin winters offer opportunities to use a snow shovel for exercise before taking the dog, June Marie, out for a walk. Her beloved husband continues to inspire stories and is a champion weed puller in the summer's garden. Together they can veggies and freeze fruit for the long winter days. Quilts and stained-glass objects made by her hands not only adorn their home but spill over into the lives of children, grandchildren, and friends galore.

Barbara Farland (p. 52) describes herself as "a writer by trade and a teacher at heart." As an award-winning communications professional and author, Barbara is credited with numerous creative works, including contributions to *Chicken Soup for the Soul, Hugs, Cup of Comfort, Short and Sweet*, and other notable anthologies.

As a Language Arts instructor with both Brightnont Academy and Art of Problem Solving (AoPS) Academy, she enjoys engaging her students with deep questions, material that taps their sense of personal meaning, opportunities for collaboration — and, of course, writing. Barbara also enjoys writing long-form lessons for Study.com, an award-winning educational platform for teachers, students, and everyone. Barbara makes her home in Minneapolis with her husband, Terry, and daughter, Nina, who graciously put up with her growing piles of books, journals, yarn, and fabric. Visit *barbarafarland.com* to learn more.

Glenda Ferguson (p. 9) holds education degrees from College of the Ozarks and Indiana University. Her work has appeared in *Angels on Earth, Chicken Soup for the Soul, Sasee,* and two volumes of the *Short and Sweet* series. Glenda also writes devotions for *All God's Creatures.* The Indiana Arts Commission included her poem "The Buffalo Trace Trail: Then and Now" in the 2021 INverse Poetry Archive.

Glenda receives encouragement from the Writers Forum of Burton Kimble Farms Education Center and her Bible Study Fellowship group. As a volunteer with Indiana Landmarks, she conducts tours of two historical hotels. Glenda and her husband Tim live on an acre in southern Indiana which they share with Speckles the cat and a variety of wildlife visitors. Since retirement, they have had more time for vacations.

Pam Groves' (p. 22) life has certainly strayed a bit from the norm. After college she moved from Portland, Oregon to teach school in an isolated rural town. She married fellow teacher, Stan, three months after they met. When their family grew to six adopted children, she chose a new role: stay-at-home mom.

Writing has been a part of Pam's life since elementary school. She says that writing for the *Short and Sweet* series has been a fun learning experience — building skills in choosing the best word and cutting what does not move the story forward. Husband Stan passed away at age 62 from microcystic adnexal carcinoma, a rare form of cancer. During their married lives, Pam and Stan took joy in their family and always trusted that God was with them.

Leah Hinton (p. 58) is a poet, short-story author, screenwriter, and playwright based in Texas. Among her awards are the McClatchy Fiction Prize for her stories *Blue*, *Dark Fog*, and *Spin-Me, Charlie*; the Poet's Prize for *Barefoot* (Dallas Area Writers), and the Audience-Choice Spotlight Award for her play, *Ripe* (2019 Stage Writers Festival).

Her play, *Paper Thin*, was a feature selection by Imprint Theatre in 2020. Her short films *Lost Man*, *Bantam*, and *Single* are in production as part of the feature-length anthology, *Dad-Father-Papa*, from Carpe Diem Pictures. Her latest screenplay to be made into a movie, *Broken Chords*, was released in 2022. She is a full member of the Dramatists Guild, Associate Director of Stage Writers, President of the Writers Guild of Texas, Event Liaison of the DFW Writers Room, and founder of R.A.W. Arts Poetry Guild.

Patricia (Patty) Huey (p. 30) was born in the Pacific Northwest but was raised in the South. After graduating from the University of Alabama, she taught school for 40 years. In 1994, she founded Hill Creek Christian School in Mount Vernon, Washington. Throughout her career, the subject she most enjoyed teaching was creative writing.

Recently, Patty and her husband completed a year living in their cabin on Dunn Mountain in the Huckleberry Range of Northeastern Washington and have moved back to Alabama. Currently, she is writing a devotional of short inspirational pieces and poetry. Her other hobbies include meeting with her Christian writers' group (Pond and Parchment Guild) via Zoom, spending time with friends and family, watching wildlife, and taking long walks with her Labrador Retriever, Liberty.

Penny L. Hunt (p. 12), award winning author, speaker, and blogger, has been published in *Chicken Soup for the Soul, Guideposts, The Upper Room,* almost every edition of the *Short and Sweet* series, and online in *Just Eighteen Summers*. Her most recent book, *Bounce! Don't Break...* helps others bounce back from setbacks. *Little White Squirrel's Secret — A Special Place to Practice,* is an Amazon.com bestseller children's book dedicated to her severely autistic granddaughter.

Penny lives in the rural-peach-growing region of South Carolina with her husband, Bill, a retired career naval officer and attaché, and their two dogs. While she enjoys gardening and gourmet cooking, her greatest passion is to lead others to a personal and intimate relationship with Christ. Visit her at PennyLHunt.com.

Debbie Jansen (p. 104) earned a Psychology degree from Evangel University, where she met Ron and began their marriage of 48 years. They have three children and six grandchildren.

Debbie has written four books, and her articles have been published in *Today's Christian Woman* and *Focus on the Family*. She has also appeared on radio and television.

She is the founder of The Family Training Center and wrote the curriculum for 120 classes. Debbie is a minister and speaker who creates videos for YouTube and produces a podcast titled "Minutes of Faith."

Debbie collects stories, information, and friends. While she loves sharing her delightful rollercoaster of life, she is also mesmerized by the adventures of others. Writing and research is her passion. Always the optimist, she never gives up until she has found answers in every difficult situation. Visit her at debbiejansen.com.

Sandra Johnson (p. 10) is a retired labor and delivery nurse and nursing instructor from Arizona. Divorced with two children and eight grandchildren, she is looking forward to welcoming her first great-grandchild very soon.

Sandra enjoys singing and is currently involved with two singing groups — one a worship team, the other a community choir of 66 members. She also teaches Bible study and is involved with her church. Traveling is another one of her passions including five cruises and a visit to the Holy Land. Recently she had the privilege to visit and camp in eight national parks in eleven days.

She loves to write and is currently working on a Christian novel about five generations of miracles. For three years, she has been an active member of Northern Arizona Word Weavers International, Cottonwood Chapter.

Debra Johnston (p. 114) writes from a fisherman's cottage on Lake Winnebago. Subjects she enjoys writing about are wetlands, birds, rivers, and the Great Lakes — anything to do with nature. She is a retired educator living in central Wisconsin with her husband and their rescue dog, a Labrador mix.

After her poem, "Oh Gentle Traveler," was featured in *Poets to Come*, a poetry anthology, she traveled to Long Island, New York, to present it at a celebration of the Walt Whitman bicentennial. She has written for *The Mailbox, The Idea Magazine for Teachers*.

She is a member of the Wisconsin Fellowship of Poets, The Society of Children Book Writers and Illustrators, and Wisconsin Wetlands Association. Follow her on X @johnstdeb and at dh-johnston.com.

Liz Kimmel (p. 16) married to Cary for 44 years, has two children and four grandchildren. She has published two books of Christian prose/poetry and a grammar workbook for middle-school students. She also has articles published in all books in the *Short and Sweet* series. Her devotions are included in Guideposts *All God's Creatures* from 2020 – 2024. She has a fiction piece in *Seasons of Change,* an anthology of the Minnesota Christian Writers Guild. Her new book, *Putting Punch in the Parables,* is a photo-illustrated, alliterative retelling of ten of the parables of Jesus. Visit her website at lizkimmelwordwright.com.

Liz provides admin support for four non-profits (Dare to Believe, Great Commission Media Ministries, the Minnesota Christian Writers Guild, and Minnesota House of Prayer). Finding time to write is challenging, but that activity brings her the greatest joy.

Born in Guatemala of missionary parents, **Debra Kornfield** (p. 25) has always been intrigued by the mysteries of human expression. During 20 years of mission work in Brazil with her husband, Dave, and four children; Debra published several books and wrote for *Cristianismo Hoje* (*Christianity Today*) and popular *Lar Cristão* (*Christian Home*). She pioneered abuse recovery, breaking taboos through her award-winning book, *Vítima, Sobrevivente, Vencedor* (*Victim, Survivor, Victor*). In 2024 she completed her Cally and Charlie historical fiction series: *Horse Thief 1898, Treasure Hunt 1904,* and *Facing the Faeries 1906.*

Debra enjoys adventuring with her grandchildren, hiking, and keeping up with her husband Dave, her seven siblings, and many South American friends. Follow her on HorseThief1898.blog and ButGod.blog.

Bob LaForge (p. 21) has been a Christian since 1977. He is married to Toni and has twin daughters, Sarah and Danielle, who were born in 2006. They all attend Grace Bible Church where Bob oversees the bookstore and teaches Adult Sunday School.

Bob has over 300 publications and has written four books which are available from Amazon: *Contemplating the Almighty* which discusses who and what God is, *Developing Great Relationships*, *The End Times and the Bible*, and a novel *The Tempter Comes*. Church Growth Institute published *Evaluating Your Friendship Skills*.

He created a website at disciplescorner.com. There, his books are available to download as well as articles, devotions, several Bible study series, and a section on Bible literacy. Tracts are also available which you can print and distribute. Everything is free.

John Leatherman (p. 98) is a writer, editor, cartoonist, writing-contest judge, word-puzzle creator, and escape-room designer. He is a longtime member and former officer of Word Weavers International (WWI), where he is a writing mentor, leads occasional seminars on self-editing, and writes a long-running grammar blog. He has won numerous writing awards from WWI, ACFW, and other organizations. He has worked with over a dozen authors to edit, proofread, rewrite, and revise their manuscripts for publication.

He also served as Communications Editor for Recode Media.

His writing credits include book reviews for *Christian Retailing*, scripts for Shoestring Radio Theater, devotionals for *Keys for Kids*, and cartoons for several magazines. He maintains a secret identity as a mild-mannered software consultant who lives in Florida and has two kids and a dog.

Allyson West Lewis (p. 96) is an award-winning author. After over 20 years as an Institutional Director on Wall Street and a Business Developer for an IT Networking company, she turned to her childhood love — writing. Allyson has been published in two previous books in the Short and Sweet series: *What's In a Name? Everything!* and *When the World Wore Masks*. She's written two speculative fiction books, and has published blog posts, short stories, and articles in literary magazines and anthologies.

In addition to teaching life skills to desperate pre-teen parents, Allyson has facilitated leadership training, served as a one-on-one mentor, and led a women's small group. She enjoys playing tennis.

She loves her amazing husband, sons, and grandchildren. Allyson writes from Hilton Head Island, South Carolina with a Golden Retriever and one irascible terrier sprawled at her feet.

Dan Lewis (p. 40) is husband to Michelle, father to college-aged sons, Nathan and Matthew, a youth minister, and a lover of God's Word. In 2015, he left his 18-year career as an electrical engineer to pursue student ministry. He also wanted to focus on time with his family — traveling and going on outdoor adventures, playing family games together, and serving together in the church and on mission trips as God calls them.

In February of 2020, 18-year-old Nathan was in a skateboarding accident that left him with a severe traumatic brain injury. Although Nathan's progress in recovery has been heartbreakingly slow, the family has experienced the love and sustaining power of Jesus in powerful ways even in the midst of this difficult season.

Kimberly Long (p. 82) loves writing, photography, mountain biking, paddle boarding, cooking, gardening, camping, fly fishing, hiking, decorating, traveling and . . . all things adventure.

Four years ago she started her own business doing window treatments and is already working on giving it over to a manager so she can start another business in photography. Her desire is to do Drone Photography , which will hopefully give her a great excuse to travel all over the world.

Kimberly has one daughter, married, and two grand babies who keep her motivated to stay fit and active. Undergoing three back surgeries 10 years ago has made Kimberly more determined to stay strong physically.

Her overriding passion is to stay not only physically but financially, mentally and spiritually fit.

Author and speaker **Terry Magness** (p. 107) is the founder of Grace Harbour Ministries, a biblically-based teaching and discipleship ministry to the nations. She is passionate to help others know the character of God and who they are in Christ, and to live victorious lives and grow to maturity in Christ, filled with His Spirit.

As an ordained Assembly of God minister, her experience in counseling and as a coach equip her to undergird and strengthen pastors and their wives, as well as credentialed women in ministry, and to encourage and empower the church.

Terry enjoys writing, photography, art, and fishing with her husband, Don. Their daughter Valarie, son Greg, daughter-in-law Jean Anne, and three granddaughters — Fallon, Savannah, and Kendall — keep them amazed, delighted, and ever thankful.

Jill Maisch (p. 94) lives in a Maryland suburb of Washington, D.C with her husband, Bill, and their two long-haired miniature dachshunds, Cooper and Bella. They feel blessed to live within a short drive of all six of their adult children and their families. Recently retired from 44 years of teaching middle-school science, Jill loves having the extra time to enjoy writing, reading, camping, bicycling, and traveling.

Other of her passions include leading cross-cultural mission experiences and, as chair of the Church and Society group at her church, being actively involved in addressing social-justice issues that impact her community.

Jill has had 12 devotions published in *The Upper Room*. "Invisible Baseball" is her sixth contribution to the *Short and Sweet* series.

Maureen Miller (p. 47) is an award-winning author and storyteller who writes for Guideposts' *All God's Creatures*. She also writes for her local newspaper, is a contributing author in numerous collaborations, and also is a featured blogger for several online devotional websites.

Maureen loves life in all its forms, enjoying it with Bill, her childhood sweetheart and husband of more than three decades, and their three "born in their hearts" children and grandchildren on Selah Farm, their hobby homestead in western North Carolina.

She blogs regularly at penningpansies.com, sharing God's extraordinary character in the ordinary things of life, and she's finishing her first novel, *Gideon's Book*, with Redemption Press. Maureen loves Jesus most, then after him all those made in His image. She also loves dogs!

Cristina Moore (p. 112) was born in Puerto Rico and grew up in Tennessee. Currently, she lives in North Carolina with her husband of over 25 years and her two younger children, twins Hope and Helena. She is the owner and CEO of Bronze Star Homes, an employee at Duke Energy, and currently serves in the North Carolina National Guard as a Brigadier General.

Cristina serves as an elder in her church and loves teaching Bible study. Cristina celebrates God's Word by sharing the grace and miracles both she and her husband have witnessed through multiple combat deployments and their call to serve their community and country. In her spare time, Cristina places family as a priority and is enjoying returning to her passion of writing and touching the lives of those reading her words.

After 30 years as a Florida adoption attorney, **Alice H. Murray** (p. 27) now pursues a different path as Operations Manager for End Game Press. With a passion for writing, she is constantly creating with words. Her work includes contributions to several *Short And Sweet* books, *The Upper Room*, *Chicken Soup for the Soul*, and the *Northwest Florida Literary Review*.

Alice is a regular contributor to *GO!*, a quarterly Christian magazine in the Florida Panhandle, and she has three devotions a month published online by Dynamic Women in Missions. Her devotions have also appeared in compilation devotionals such as *Ordinary People Extraordinary God* (July 2023) and Guideposts' *Pray A Word A Day, Vol. 2* (June 2023). Alice's first book, *Secrets at Chimneys*, an annotated Agatha Christie mystery, was released in April 2023.

Suzanne Dodge Nichols (p. 64) is a 2021 Selah Awards recipient and a 2022 and 2024 Selah Awards finalist. She is published in eight books of the *Short and Sweet* series and in the 2021, 2022, and 2023 *Divine Moments* Christmas anthologies. She is a contributor to *Day by Day: 40 Devotionals for Writers & Creative Types* and *A Memoir of Mothers*. She is also a co-author of the numerous-award-winning *COFFEE with God*, volumes 1-4.

Suzanne and her husband make their home in Hartselle, Alabama. They have three children and ten grandchildren who live *much* too far away.

Theresa Parker Pierce (p. 76) lives in Historic Salisbury, North Carolina, where she enjoys spending time with family and friends. She has 35 years of experience teaching reading and history in both private and public schools. A graduate of East Carolina University, Theresa has a Master's degree in education from Catawba College and is National Board-certified. Two-time Rowan Salisbury Teacher of the Year, she enjoys storytelling about her childhood in eastern North Carolina and the history of Rowan County.

Theresa is a member of Word Weavers International, Blue Ridge Christian Writers, Room at the Table, and the 540 Writing Club. She writes monthly for *Senior Savvy* magazine. She shares her volunteer time between the North Carolina Transportation Museum in Spencer and the Rowan Museum in Salisbury. Theresa speaks for schools and civic groups.

Sue Rice (p. 19) began authoring short stories when she lost her twin sister eight years ago and wrote about that experience. *Guideposts Magazine* published her first story. Since that time, she has been published in a number of magazines and anthologies. Her letters to the editor have been published in Epoch Times and her local paper.

Since retiring as an HR Director, Sue has taught ESL for six years and enjoys watching her children and grandchildren become who God meant them to be. She and her husband of 54 years love to travel, spend time with family, and watch the antics of their four-footed "kids" — a dog and a cat. Sue also works with Braver Angels, a nationwide organization whose mission is to heal the divide in our country.

On her website, heathernroberts.com, **Heather Roberts** (p. 80) writes about encouraging insights she receives from the Lord. She's also on Instagram at heather.n.roberts, and on Facebook. Heather has been blessed to write for Focus on the Family, Guideposts, Christian devotions, Grace publishing, *Prayer Connect*, *The Secret Place*, *Unlocked*, Cross River Media, and more. She works as a pediatric occupational therapist in the school system. Heather attends a church that actively seeks the hurt and lost via outreach ministries. She also leads several local and international prayer groups.

Heather is the mother of four and wife to an amazing husband. Chocolate is her archnemesis, and she cherishes time spent in pursuing God. Often she can be found scoping out people's landscaping and dreaming of adding another garden.

Beverly Robertson (p. 110) recalls that her high school English class first sparked her interest in writing. Fellow students selected her essay "Teachers" to be published in the local paper. Stories smoldered in a file cabinet until her retirement from a position as a teacher's aide in an elementary school. Then her writing ignited.

She pulled out her stories on biblical women, put them together in an anthology, and self-published the book *Bible Brides: Trials and Triumphs*. For her church's women's group, she presented a monthly lesson on different women of the Bible. She has had a short story appear in *Whatever Lovely* magazine and Christmas stories in *Celebrating Christmas* and *Christmas Spirit*. She networks and hones her writing skills as a member of the American Christian Fiction Writers.

Kim Robinson (p. 56) just loves Jesus' "kisses" from heaven — the ways in which He touches her day with helps, gifts, wise words, and friends. For years she taught grades 6-12, mostly English and math, in Oregon and Alaska. Then God called her on a grand trip, and she moved to a hospital ship that served West African ports with hope and surgeries. She taught the missionary children onboard, mostly the subjects of English and Bible, from 2007 until COVID shut the work down in 2020.

Today, Kim lives in Oregon with her cat, Peanut, where she writes, hikes, sews quilts, and reads (a lot). Her daughter's family in Montana and her son from Los Angeles delight her. Kim is a member of Cascade Christian Writers and often serves as an editor and writer for missionaries.

Martha Rogers (p. 92) is a southern girl who thrives on encouraging others to discover true joy and freedom in the richness of God's unending grace and mercy. The mother of two grown daughters adopted from China makes her home in Alachua, Florida with her husband, Doug. She currently directs a group of ladies called Sweet Notes who sing monthly at local nursing homes.

As a member of Word Weavers, Martha loves writing Christian devotions. She has been published in the *Whispers of Grace* anthology and the *Short and Sweet* series. Through her battle with depression, she hopes to write her story of how God took her from the pit of darkness into the light of His freedom and joy.

Newly retired as a high school career & technology education teacher, **Desiree St. Clair Spears** (p. 102) has 30 years of experience teaching all ages from infant to adult. She earned her M.A. at Notre Dame of Maryland University and her B.S. at Salisbury University. She is active in her church, serving as a trustee, greeter, and leader of a women's small group.

Desiree has written for numerous publications including *Guideposts*, the *Short and Sweet* series, *A Joy-Full Season*, *The Times-Crescent* newspaper, and her church blog. Recently, she celebrated her first anniversary with her husband, Robert, and is the mother of three adult children and grandmother of eleven. In addition to spoiling the grandkids, she enjoys traveling, hiking, and life on the farm. Her blog can be viewed at desireeglass.blogspot.com.

Pastor and retired USAF chaplain **Jack Stanley** (p. 78) has been called to minister to troops in central California, Alabama, Washington D.C., Las Vegas, northern Italy, Oxford, England, and in a deployed setting to South West Asia, Iraq, Afghanistan, and many others locations that must remain unnamed. His first book, *Stand Strong: Spiritual Resilience the Ephesians Way* was published in 2012, and he is a weekly columnist for his local newspaper.

For 31 years Jack has been married to a teacher of British literature who helps him improve his writing skills. They have a daughter just in college and a son just out of it, both whom publish blogs. He has performed as a musician around the world, and enjoys writing, sports, the arts, and all that God makes beautiful.

The Rev. Dr. Judson I. Stone (p. 89) is the author of a biography of his father, *A Last Chapter of the Greatest Generation* (2016). His biography of a great-great uncle, *A Modest But Crucial Hero,* was published in 2023.

Judson volunteers at the Walton Correctional Institution in DeFuniak Springs, Florida, and at his church in Santa Rosa Beach. Judson served as a pastor for 26 years in Maine. He is also retired from being a corporate chaplain in Arlington, Texas, where he volunteered as a sports chaplain in high school football and college basketball. He has also taught Bible courses in Hyderabad, India.

Judson is married and the father of three grown sons, and grandfather of five grandchildren. He is a member of the Destin Word Weavers International chapter.

Shelli Virtue (p. 50) grew up a pastor's kid, graduated from Pillsbury Baptist Bible college with a BS in Bible, homeschooled her 4 children, is a full-time caregiver to her disabled adult son, and was the vice-president of a youth center. She enjoys being Gran to three adorable grandsons.

Shelli is the author of Bible studies. Her deep desire is to encourage improved relationships with God and others through her thought-provoking studies and weekly emails. She asks difficult questions and is open to creative ways of thinking in her approach to better her relationship with God and others. Her studies include: *The Road to Relationship: A Journey through the Book of Matthew*, *Humility: The Insight into God's Kingdom*, *Unpacking Your Pain: Complete Healing through Lamentations*, and *A CURE for Good Intentions: Lessons from 13 Everyday Guys*.

Judith Vander Wege (p. 70) is a Christian freelance writer/composer and Bible study leader. She has been published in 300+ Christian periodicals and a newspaper. Formerly a registered nurse, piano teacher, bookkeeper, and para educator, she earned a Bachelor of Arts in music ministry as a senior citizen. She lives in Orange City, Iowa and attends First Reformed Church. Her passion is to help hurting people grow into an intimate relationship with God, to experience His love and healing.

Judith has recently published four books: *Rescued By God's Mercy*, *Songs & Poems From a Yielded Heart*, *The Runaway: A Parable to Show How God Feels About Rebellion*, and *Blessed Through the Years*, a compilation of short stories and articles.

Connect with Judith through her website: judithvanderwege.com, or her email: judith.vw.4hm@gmail.com.

Kenneth Avon White (p. 116) was first published in 2013 in the devotional publication, *The Upper Room*. His first short story was published by Grace Publishing in their anthology *Short & Sweet: Small Words for Big Thoughts*. More recently, his short story, "Provision Awaits on the Other Side," was published in Guideposts 2023 book, *Exploring God's Promises: Hope*," and his meditation "Doubt," appeared in their 2023 book, *Pray a Word for Hope*.

Ken resides in Gastonia, North Carolina and is an organizational change manager for the Lowe's corporation. In his spare time he takes in the robust Charlotte cultural scene and ponders the question, "With the limited time I have, do I finally get to write that first novel or head to the gym to shed the COVID gift that keeps on giving — 30 extra pounds?"

Susan Cheeves King

For nearly four decades, Susan King has been a fish out of water — a big extrovert serving in professions dominated by introverts: writer, college teacher, and editor. During her nearly 25 years as an editor with *The Upper Room* magazine, Susan taught and mentored writers at over 100 Christian writers' conferences in the US and Canada.

While teaching English and feature-writing classes over a span of 27 years at Lipscomb, Biola, and Abilene Christian Universities, her greatest challenge and joy was to help each of her over 4,000 students become the epitome of an educated person: someone who can think well, speak well, and write well.

These days, she pursues her passion through Susan King Editorial Services (www.susankingedits.com) by editing, and mentoring writers and also by teaching and helping writers perfect their craft at writers' conferences. She and husband, Joe, live in middle Tennessee — very close to two of their grown children and their two grandsons.

If you enjoyed

[this title]

you might also enjoy
other books in the *Short and Sweet* Series

Short and Sweet
Small Words for Big Thoughts

Short and Sweet Too
More Small Words for Big Thoughts

The Short and Sweet of It
When the Right Word Is a Short Word

Short and Sweet Goes Fourth

Short and Sweet Takes the Fifth

Family Album

A Different Beat

Humili8ing
Tales We Wish Weren't True

Angels in Disguise?

What's in a Name? Everything!

When the World Wore Masks

Grace Publishing Anthologies

If you're a writer with a story to tell, consider submitting your work for inclusion in upcoming books in a Grace Publishing anthology.

Short and Sweet Series

Each book in the *Short and Sweet* series is a labor of love, so no one is compensated monetarily. Authors share with the possibility of changing someone's life, heart, or mind. All royalties from this series go to World Christian Broadcasting, a non-profit organization whose purpose is to take God's Word — through mass media — to people who may have no other means of hearing the Good News. However each of the authors whose work is selected to be published will receive a free copy of the book and a discount on orders.

For this book series we use words of only one syllable in the stories related to the book's theme.

Seven exceptions to the one-syllable-word-only requirement:

1. Any proper noun is okay. (If you were born in California, don't write Maine; if a name is Machenheimer, don't write Clark.)
2. You may use polysyllabic words of 5 letters or fewer — for example: into, over, area, about.
3. You may use contractions of more than one syllable such as couldn't, wouldn't, didn't.
4. You may use numbers (even those that are polysyllabic).
5. As in any published work, direct quotes — even in casual conversation — must be rendered word-for-word as they occurred, so their wording is exempt from the rules. This includes verses from the Bible — but only translations, not paraphrases (such as *The Message*).
6. Multi-syllable words for family (for which there are no single-syllable synonyms) are fine: mother, father, family, sister, brother, sibling, husband, daughter, relative etc.
7. Words for which no synonym exists — such as college/university, heredity, communication, integrity, honest/honesty, person, regret, career/profession, passion, destination, hospital, education/ teacher/professor, institution, creativity, identity — or that cannot be replaced by a natural-sounding phrase of simple, one-syllable words.

Writers often find it easier to write the story, then go back and replace the words that don't meet the series' requirements.

The general purpose of your piece is to entertain — rather than to teach or merely inform — so the tone should be personal and optimistic rather than instructive.

Both multi-published and beginning or non-published authors write for the series. Stories may be original or previously published if rights have been returned (as long as we are informed of the latter in advance). Grace Publishing retains rights after acceptance until publication, then rights automatically return to the author.

The article length is anywhere from 250-1,000 words. Previous books have included poems. The main point is the context of the story. (Take a look at previous *Short and Sweet* books that Grace Publishing has released.)

Submissions should be Times New Roman, 12-point type, sent as a Microsoft Word attachment to an email. Subject line should include the title of the book. In the header at the top of the submission, include: your name, mailing address for the one free copy, your email address and the story's word count.

Please include with your submission a clear, crisp, 300 ppi/dpi color headshot (as an attachment in jpeg format) and a a bio of no less than 100 and no more than125 words. Each writer's photo and bio will appear in the About the Author section at the end of the book.

Send to Susan King: shortandsweettoo@gmail.com.

Short and Sweet Is Accepting Submissions for the Following Titles for 2024-2025

Memorable Mutts

The Feline in the Family

Facing Fears: Facing and conquering fears big or small, whether as a child or an adult.

Divine Moments

Divine Moments is an award-winning series. Each book is a labor of love, so no one is compensated monetarily. Authors share with the possibility of changing someone's life, heart, or mind. All royalties from this series go to Samaritan's Purse, an organization that helps victims of war, poverty, natural disasters, disease, and famine with the purpose of sharing God's love through His son, Jesus Christ. However, each of the authors whose work is selected to be published will receive a free copy of the book and a discount on orders.

Send your personal articles! The story is the important thing. The article length is anywhere from 500-2,000 words. Previous books have included poems and even some pieces written by children, so the guidelines aren't strict. The main point is the context of the story. (Take a look at previous Moments books that Grace Publishing has released, particularly the first one, *Divine Moments,* for examples.)

Both multi-published and beginning or non-published authors write for the series. Stories may be original or previously published if rights have been returned (as long as we are informed of the latter in advance). Grace Publishing retains rights after acceptance until publication, then rights automatically return to the author.

Submissions should be Times New Roman, 12-point type, sent as a Microsoft Word attachment to an email. Subject line should include the title of the book. Please include in the header at the top of the submission: your name, mailing address for the one free copy, your email address and the story's word count. Also include with your submission a bio of 100-125 words. Each writer's bio will appear in the About the Author section at the end of the book. Send to Terri Kalfas: terri@grace-publishing.com.

Divine Moments Is Accepting Submissions for the Following Titles

Questionable Moments: Whether these stories are serious or funny, they should be the "What was I thinking?" type of story. They might even address whether the questionable behavior was redeemed or even redeemable, and why or why not.

Favorite Moments: Personal stories of times that bring a smile to your face whenever you think of them, and will make others smile, too.

Divine Detours: Stories that show how your personal plans/goals/actions were changed because of God's movement in your life, the way you responded during the experience, and when or how you realized God was in control and "behind" it all.

Unexpected Kindness: These should be stories of a time in your life when you received unexpected or undeserved kindness/grace from others.

Patriotic Moments: These stories go beyond the typical school essays from childhood. They are stories of actions that exemplify true personal love and celebration of the U.S.

Hopeful Moments: These stories should be uplifting. They can include (but are not limited to) what hope and hopefulness means to you, seasons of hope you have experienced, and stories of times when all hope seemed lost until. . . .

Christmas 2024 (as yet untitled)

www.ingramcontent.com/pod-product-compliance
Lightning Source LLC
Chambersburg PA
CBHW070458100426
42743CB00010B/1665